AF259301

The 'Plenty' Book: the Answer to the Question: "What Can I do to Make This a Better World?"
Copyright © 2019 by Stephen P. Watkins.

All rights reserved. No part of this book may be reproduced in any form or by any electronic or mechanical means including information storage and retrieval systems, without permission in writing from the author. The only exception is by a reviewer, who may quote short excerpts in a review.

Cover designed by Stephen P. Watkins

Stephen P. Watkins

Printed in the United States of America

First Printing: 2019.
Independently Published.

ISBN-978-1-7333984-0-4

*The most common way people give up
their power
is by thinking they don't have any.*

\--- Alice Walker

DISCLAIMER

The collection of ideas, philosophies, and concepts from various authors forms an important part of this book. In good faith, this book contains fair use of copyrighted materials as provided under 17 U.S.C. § 107 of the U.S. Copyright Law.

Section 107 of the U.S. Copyright Law on "Fair Use" provides a list of various purposes for which the use of a particular work may be considered fair, such as criticism, comment, news reporting, teaching, scholarship and research. Copyright protects the particular way an author has expressed himself. It does not extend to any ideas, systems, or factual information conveyed in the work.

The use of a small portion of various authors' works has been done in a non-competitive way in order to educate the readers and bring to their attention the authors' original works. Readers are invited to refer back to the authors' original works (all references have been provided herein). The purpose is to illustrate the point made in this book, and, more importantly, to benefit and educate the public and bring to their attention the huge amount of knowledge, ideas, concepts and information that the original authors have accumulated throughout the years in their own areas of expertise.

DEDICATION

I dedicate this book to my mother, Pauline Snipes Watkins Koch. She had the kindest heart of anyone I ever knew, and devoted so much of her life to making this a better world when she left it than when she entered it. She taught me to care about others, to recognize that the only things that count are the things you can't count, to care for Mother Earth and to cherish the values that protect and nourish Her, so we can be protected and nourished. She spent much time and money and energy and care fighting to protect the environment, the values that make this a better society, and helping to give hope to the hopeless. Mom, I miss you. This book comes from my heart, and is a tribute to your memory. May it benefit the world as you have blessed me with life, laughter, and love. . . .

PREFACE

SCADS OF PEOPLE WERE SHOCKED BY THE ELECTION OF Donald J. Trump to the Presidency of the United States on November 8, 2016. Some felt that the country had finally gotten a leader they could look up to, while others felt that the end times were here. More than a few hunkered down to see what would happen during the next four years. All agreed that this was a President unlike any seen in our history and that the face of America, as seen through the eyes of the world, had changed dramatically. Few could foresee the spate of Tweets emanating from the President's White House restroom at 3:00 A.M.

Thought leaders on both the right and left sides of the American political spectrum have expressed strong beliefs in why their side was right, and the other side was wrong. Right and wrong about what?

Pundits, bloggers, and average people would agree that our country is more divided than ever. There are strong, widening trends pushing us to more calcified positions on the right and the left. Questions have arisen regarding the direction we should take on culture; education; the economy and jobs; the military; foreign relations; the environment; science and technology; faith; the size and nature of government; politics; and America's future in a dramatically changing world. The talking heads have managed to co-opt the macro-discussion to suit their own purposes, and by distilling their strongest arguments into print or televised talking points, they have managed to cast themselves into the roles of "expert" on their topic *de jour*.

Of key significance is the fact that our society has changed many values, practices and traditions over the years, and as each side has hardened its position, it becomes more difficult to find a basis on which people can work together to face and overcome common problems. Indeed, it is the very hardening of positions that make it difficult for people on one side of an issue to recognize that those on the other side may have different perspectives that just might lead to solutions. We used to honor those who mastered the art of compromise, and based our society, in all its many aspects, on the notion of give-and-take. Nowadays, the increasingly brittle and mutually-hostile establishment of "positions" makes compromise a forgotten art form, and yet it is essential in order to survive this increasingly-fraught world.

The frequently-heard response heard by this author to the question of "what can be done to make this a better world?" is "nothing. I'm just one person. What could I possibly do to improve things?"

After many years of thought and involvement in political, environmental, and social groups, I have come up with a resounding, one-word answer:

Plenty

PEOPLE NOW TAKE A CYNICAL VIEW OF THE MOTIVATIONS of those on the other side of the political spectrum. The right-wingers, with their sneering disregard for the people trying to level the playing field, make snide comments about the goals of those in the groups trying to help immigrants, low-income workers, health-afflicted people, those suffering from racism, or those in the lesbian-gay-bisexual-transgender community. The left-wingers, many of whom are Millennials, often display excessively sensitive political correctness, making put-down comments about the ignorant, socially- and culturally rigid views of the right-wingers, accusing them of racism and other forms of bigotry and social intolerance.

The point is this: when people focus on their differences, that is all they see. "What you focus on expands." We need communities of like-minded people willing to work together—-despite their so-called differences—-to face and overcome common problems. When we have such groups working together, we have a chance to make this a much better neighborhood, city, state, country, and, yes, a better Planet Earth.

As Carl Sagan famously put it, "This little blue-green ball, a mote suspended in a sunbeam, is our home." From a fact-based perspective, it is not reasonable to focus on terra-forming Mars or inhabiting the moons of Jupiter or Saturn as humanity's new abode. We need to learn how to live together in ways that provide guidance for personal growth, but within the boundaries of society. When we can learn to do that, then we will have created the foundation for Heaven on Earth.

Although there is much social and political commentary in this book, its purpose is not to provoke arguments, but to find solutions that won't go out of date in the next month or year. Instead, the real goal is to show evergreen solutions that will make sense now, a year from now, a decade from now, and maybe longer.

And so, when people ask, "What can be done?," I respond "Plenty!"

ACKNOWLEDGEMENTS

There are many people in my life who have encouraged, supported, and uplifted me. The ones who cared the most provided me with strong, constructive criticism; helped me look at things from different perspectives; and encouraged me to challenge myself to be the best human being I could be.

I have tried to give credit and sources whenever and wherever possible. I truly thank all those people who assiduously worked on the process of helping me to get out my message in the form of this book. It is not my intention to overlook anyone, but the list of all the people who have helped me over the years is simply too long to go into here. Their contributions are phenomenal, and deeply appreciated. To those still alive, you know who you are. To those who have passed on, I honor your spirits by emulating them in words and deeds.

Should anyone find any errors in this work, please know that they are strictly mine; I own them.

The person most deserving of my deepest love and appreciation for all of these things, and more, is Susan Mesrobyan. She came into my life at a time when I was emotionally vulnerable and in need of an abiding kind of love; she gave me the support that helped me overcome some real challenges; and now we have a loving family which accepts me for who I am, warts and all.

Thank you, Susan, from the bottom of my heart.

PART I
POLITICS AND THE LAW

CHAPTER 1
THE BIOLOGY OF POLITICS

"Man is by nature a social animal; an individual who is unsocial naturally and not accidentally is either beneath our notice or more than human. Society is something that precedes the individual. Anyone who either cannot lead the common life or is so self-sufficient as not to need to and therefore does not partake of society, is either a beast or a god." — Aristotle, *Politics*

I GREW UP IN A FAMILY that was all about politics.

As a child of two progressive parents who cut his political teeth on being exposed to the socialists who gathered at the First Unitarian-Universalist Church of Los Angeles in the 1950s and 1960s, I grew up in an admittedly-unusual family.

My earliest memories were about my parents' involvement at the Unitarian Church in the mid-1950s. My stepfather, Donald E. Koch, originally from Montréal, moved to Los Angeles in 1948. Shortly after his arrival, he had to register with the Selective Service. In June 1950, the United States entered the Korean War. My stepdad was drafted. He was a conscientious objector, based not on religious grounds but on political principles. He thought the Korean War was an illegal "police action." He fought in court, but lost, and was sentenced to spend three and a half years in McNeill Island Federal Penitentiary off the coast of Washington State.

By the time my stepdad returned to Los Angeles in 1954, the anti-Communist hysteria was in full swing. McCarthyism, the "Hollywood 10" witch hunts, the paranoia about Soviet infiltration, were pervasive. Koch was viewed as a hero in the Unitarian Church, where he assumed the chairmanship of the Unitarian Fellowship for Social Justice. My mother was its secretary, and together they organized presentations by members of the Hollywood 10 and other liberals/progressives who were under attack by the FBI and other parts of the government.

Koch was a great reader, as was my mother, and they clearly shared many values. Eventually, they got married on January 8, 1956, and the great San Francisco attorney and 1952 Progressive Party presidential candidate, Vincent Hallinan, was Koch's best man. (They were both alumni of McNeill.)

During the 1950s, being suspected of having left-of-center political views could get you in a world of trouble. My stepdad was no exception to this rule. He was a degreed engineer from prestigious McGill University in Montréal, but couldn't keep a job due to the FBI following him and asking questions of his employers. My mother, a legal secretary, wound up as the breadwinner for the family, working in law offices during the day and taking on evening and weekend work as a typist and publisher. She had multiple typewriters and a mimeograph machine and would prepare and mail newsletters for different progressive organizations, along with two or three authors for whom she worked as a publicist.

This situation put almost unbearable stress on my mother, and I remember many fierce arguments between her and my stepdad, often occurring late at night. My stepdad did not know how to raise me, and so, on weekends when my mother was in law offices or otherwise working, he would literally spend hours lecturing me on the great wrongs in this society and how appalling its improper values were.

He would smoke cigarettes and drink multiple cups of coffee, venting at me as if I were a willing, masochistic member of his audience. Sadly, as a frightened, five year-old child, I had no power to refuse his rants, and had to put up with them for a long time. I never told my mother because my stepfather was a big, imposing man, and used to boast about his days as a successful boxer during his time at McGill University. I was afraid that he would beat us up, and maybe kill us.

By the year 1962, the McCarthyist qualities of American political life had diminished somewhat. In early August of that year, my younger half-brother, Raymond, was born. His birth softened my stepdad's pedantic style very slightly, although he still lectured me on Saturdays and/or Sundays whenever the chance presented itself.

What I remember from the mid-1950s until the birth of my kid brother was the exercise of power: power in society, wielded by the right-wingers in political office, and power in my family, wielded by my stepdad, who had a bad temper, a mountain of frustrations, and no ability to empathize with or display fatherly feelings for me.

Thus, at an early age I learned that politics is all about power, especially the animalistic kind. How so? If you look at rivalries in the animal kingdom, you inevitably see battles of tooth and claw, forces which rule the animal kingdom. The same holds true with human beings, albeit on a much deadlier level.

I started with Politics and the Law based on some fundamental truths about human beings. In many ways, humans exist only a few paces outside the "mouth of the cave," so to speak. Like our chimpanzee and bonobo cousins (with whose DNA we share 98.8%), we have certain hard-wired genetic tendencies whose effects have had profoundly dangerous consequences for our species for hundreds of thousands of years. It is what I call the "compare-and-envy" gene, and in the vast majority of self-unaware humans, this tendency makes us look at what others have and feel prehensile, envious, and insecure.

This genetic predisposition has led to some appalling and species-threatening attitudes: "Us versus Them," dehumanization, religious, racial, cultural, sexual oriented, and gender-based discrimination and violence, up to and including genocide.

These views arise from the unaware (and uncontrolled) manifestations of what has long been called activities of the "reptilian brain," described as part of the so-called "triune brain theory." This analysis is derived from American physician and neuroscientist Paul D. McLean's tripartite brain model of the evolution of the forebrain of vertebrates, his thesis going back more than 50 years. Although the triune model of the mammalian brain including ours is viewed by some comparative neuroscientists as an oversimplified organizing theme, nonetheless it allows for certain broadly-significant descriptions of the sources of brain activity.

For example, the ability to think in abstract terms, to plan, to organize, to look to the future, to engage in simulation, derive from the activities of the neocortex, that part of the brain clusters newest (and least developed) among *homo sapiens.*

The "limbic brain" refers to those brain structures, wherever located, associated with social and nurturing behaviors, mutual reciprocity, and other behaviors and effects that arose during the age of the mammals. The actions based on limbic brain activities have led to group survival; self-sacrifice for the sake of others; caring, giving and taking for sustainable relationships; and empathic feelings. The parental instinct is perhaps the strongest exhibit of the limbic brain's influence on human behavior.

The "reptilian brain" refers to those brain structures related to territoriality, ritual behavior and other "reptile" behaviors. It is action in this part of the brain—-primarily, the *amygdala*——which has led to considerable hostility, not only between individuals but between groups. Sexual aggression and externalized hostility are linked in many studies to excessive activity in the *amygdalae,* and to imbalances in the size of these parts of the brain.

Although there may have been apparent survival value in prehumans' displays of reptilian brain activity, that is, hyper-aggression, inter-tribal warfare, and doubt, distrust, and fear, those attitudes are extraordinarily dangerous in the age of nuclear weapons. Despite our knowledge of these characteristics' dangers, they persist.

Even thousands of years ago, during the time of the ancient civilizations in the Middle East, India, and China, it was found that if people were to live together and survive, they would have to put aside their differences and live under laws.

Those laws derived from some form of politics, the obtaining and wielding and administering of power. In prehistoric times, politics was not more complicated than "might makes right." The family head became the clan head became the tribal head. As society's structures became more complex, a more sophisticated form of leadership developed to cope with greater social intricacy. Instead of relying solely on brute force, a king or his equivalent would get power by any means available; intrigue was the motto of monarchs as the centuries passed.

The larger the population, and the more sophisticated its structure, the more it became necessary to embody the ruler's edicts and fiats into bodies of law. The *Code of Hammurabi*, some 3,800 years old, is deemed to be the earliest written codification of laws. From that point, going forward, pharaohs, kings, emperors, caesars, shahs, khans and the like specified their rules of behavior for thousands of years.

More recently, societies gradually began to adopt democracy as the form of government best suiting humanity. Not every nation adopted this belief, of course, but many did, and others strive (or claim to attempt) to achieve some version of democracy in their countries' political configuration.

Broadly speaking, the types of government have evolved over the millennia, from family, to clan, to tribal, to city-state, to enclaves of nobility within a monarchy, to a "pure" monarchy, to democracy. Factors making up the shift from one form of government to the other have involved religion, military victories (or defeats), family alliances, and the economy.

As an organism evolves into greater complexity, its brain naturally has to evolve to properly control the body. Without a corresponding neural evolution, the host organism will eventually be unable to compete in the world, and will die.

The increasing complexity of the brain was needed to assert greater power to control the disparate elements of the body. Likewise, a more complex body of laws (rules and regulations to which obedience was required, by force of authority, if necessary) had to be enacted, either by a governing body or by monarchical decree, to ensure that people acted in accordance with the government's policies.

Some laws were created through representatives' votes, others by religious or regal command, but regardless of the form of government, nations' powers are developed through politics, and their means of creating rules of behavior come from laws. That is why I started this book with the structure of the means of acquiring and manifesting power, and the rules by which we live. Without a coherent strategy for acquiring and administering resources that was more or less sustainable, a society would quickly destroy itself and life would be reduced to what Thomas Hobbes described in *Leviathan* as the State of Nature, in which

---

> "the natural condition of mankind is what would exist if there were no government, no civilization, no laws, and no common power to restrain human nature. ... Life in the state of nature is solitary, poor, nasty, brutish and short."

CHAPTER 2
A LITTLE HISTORY

As a small child, with no friends, I retreated from a highly-stressful family life into the world of reading. I loved paleontology, of course, as so many little kids love dinosaurs, but my great literary love was history. It was in my immersion in history that I found relief from the tensions around me. I especially loved American history.

In America's pre-Revolution days, a significant resentment had built up against the British government. Heavy-handed, draconian in many respects, the English rulers had a view of their colonial subjects as *instrumentum vocale*, "talking tools." Barely- or uneducated, most colonists worked as farmers and continued to suffer the miserable lives that their English ancestors had experienced for hundreds of years. They lived, served, and died in obeisance to their colonial masters.

However, this period in history, from roughly 1620 through the French Revolution in 1789, was known as the Age of Enlightenment, when philosophers such as Beccaria, Diderot, Hume, Kant, Montesquieu, Rousseau, Adam Smith, and Voltaire adopted, discussed, and published ideas based on Reason and Science, rather than blind obedience to the Church and the Monarchy.

Using the works of earlier philosophers such as Bacon, Descartes, Locke, and Spinoza from the 1600s, the later writers believed in liberty, progress, tolerance, fraternity, constitutional government and separation of church and state. In France, the central doctrines of the Enlightenment philosophers were individual liberty and religious tolerance, in opposition to an absolute monarchy and the fixed dogmas of the Roman Catholic Church.

These ideas crossed the Atlantic and began to be discussed and adopted by England's American cousins. In January 1776, the "Father of the American Revolution," Thomas Paine, wrote *Common Sense*, an extraordinarily-popular pamphlet spread throughout the 13 colonies. In it, he captured the widespread spirit of resentment against King George III, as well as the corrupt British government, fomented dissent against the abuses of colonialism as well as the Crown's tyrannical rule, and urged independence and freedom for the two million colonists living in America.

The Founding Fathers did not have huge libraries, but they had enough literature to help them understand the fundamental concepts of governance throughout the ages. Ranging from Aristotle's *Politics* to Voltaire's *The Historical Praise of Reason*, they read, thought about, digested, discussed, and eventually synthesized the principles of democracy that would lead to the Articles of Confederation and, ultimately, the Constitution.

Many great ideas abounded in the Declaration of Independence, the Articles of Confederation, and the Constitution, but what was particularly brilliant was the concept of checks and balances, to serve as the braking force that would prevent the rise of a tyrant or allow majority rule to suppress the rights of the minority.

It was the balancing of competing interests, in a socio-political framework consisting of multiple diverse viewpoints of how society should be politically structured, which provided the Constitution with the power to help us overcome our selfish, "reptilian brain" impulses, and to work towards a more civilized existence as a nation.

I define democracy as "the harmonization of interests for the sake of the interests being harmonized." That was the goal of the rationalist Founders, such as George Washington, Thomas Jefferson, and James Madison, who thought of human relations as being susceptible to the logical balancing that their Deist theology encompassed.

If harmonization of competing interests was our objective, then the Constitution would serve as the mechanism that would provide us with the means to achieve it, albeit imperfectly.

By instituting a political structure through the country's organic document---the Constitution---which created a set of dominant laws that would guide us in forming and running three branches of government, its Framers built a solid foundation on which our more local, i.e., state, county, and municipal, laws would rest. The operations of the brachial divisions, i.e., the executive, legislative, and judicial, were structured in such a way as to provide counterbalancing force so that each branch would be subject to the restraints of the other two.

Although the Constitution was presented to the Constitutional Convention in Philadelphia in the period from May 25 through September 17, 1787, and it was signed on September 17, it had to be ratified by no less than nine of the 13 colonies. On March 4, 1789, New Hampshire became the 9th state to ratify it, and that was the date the Constitution became effective.

What many people today view as the most important part of the Constitution is the Bill of Rights, written mostly by James Madison (who borrowed heavily from the Virginia Declaration of Rights, written by George Mason two months before the Declaration of Independence).

The Bill of Rights, collectively, is the group of the first 10 Amendments to the Constitution. These rights provide for everything fundamental to our concept of liberty as Americans, ranging from freedom of the press to limitations on the federal power in favor of states' rights.

When the Bill of Rights was finally ratified on December 15, 1791, our Constitution was the harbinger of an exciting era, one full of great possibilities for a new age of Man.

The "new age," of course, was full of significant imperfections.

African-Americans were the victims of slavery; Indians, of genocide; and women were treated as mindless chattels.

Our view of diversity then was much more primitive than it is now. It was understood in a very superficial way: "diversity" was often seen through superficial distinctions based on external appearances, rather than looking at the intrinsic characteristics of people, places, or things.

Likewise, we operated at the time of the country's foundation on the basis of two myths: one, the Myth of Superabundance, and two, the Myth of Scientific Supremacy (these two terms were coined by Stewart Udall, in his seminal work *The Quiet Crisis*). Whatever went wrong, so the reasoning went, Man could fix through the application of rational, scientific principles.

Based on the idealism of the Enlightenment, and coupled with ignorance of what lay ahead of us, we viewed our historical path as one which would later be called "Manifest Destiny." We thought there was unlimited natural abundance in North America, which gave us the excuse to plunder, pollute, abandon, and move on.

At the turn of the 19th Century, we really had no idea of the physical dimensions of America or the magnitude of its resources. Our crude, overbearing spirit treated the Indians despicably, and, in 1830, our seventh President, Andrew Jackson, a slave-holding plantation owner, signed the *Indian Removal Act*, which legislated genocidal treatment of Native Americans and resulted in the tragic Trail of Tears.

From that point, American politics began to resemble our more modern political system. Jackson founded the Democratic Party. Patronage was the pillar of both Republican and Democratic campaigning for many years, from the 1830s up to the 1930s, and political corruption was blatant on both sides of the aisle to that time.

CHAPTER 3
TODAY'S POLITICS

Today, patronage is a bird of a different feather: instead of bribing voters through big-city "machines," or promises of free land and other trimmings to accompany it, nowadays politicians rely heavily on large campaign contributions through the monied class, e.g., the Sheldon Adelsons, the Koch brothers, the Mercers, the DeVos family, and many others of their ilk. The politicians use money to buy lots of advertising and to get their chosen candidate elected.

I remember in some of the local political contests in the 1960s and early 1970s that campaign workers would line up after a successful election, with their hands out and a fervid desire to board the gravy train of patronage appointments. They would inevitably talk about how they "delivered" this church congregation or that *equipo del barrio* (neighborhood team) and thus deserved a place in the elected official's staff.

The patronage appointments of today arise because of the demands to repay campaign debts; the needs to assuage key constituencies; or obtain legislative support through the shrewd distribution of jobs. Presidents, governors, and mayors follow this practice throughout the country.

Focused advertising is full of promises to the candidate's target electorate. The less-sophisticated voters often tend to believe the promises made by the politicians: more jobs, lower taxes, better treatment for "us," harsher treatment of "them," and many other promises of benefits that would be transparently absurd if these low-information people had the ability or the willingness to think critically.

The more progressive voters tend to be better educated and are not nearly as susceptible to the perfidious promises of politicians as their poorly-educated, semi- or illiterate "country cousins." Many of the conservative voters believe in "civil religion," a la the late Billy Graham's teachings; have bigoted/racist attitudes toward non-white people; and hold simplistic (unrealistic) views of our national economy and its interrelatedness with the world economy. The "cultural Southerners" adhere to values wherein the ownership, possession, and use of guns are exalted; "manly" sports (e.g., football, NASCAR racing, motocross) are given top-billing among the sports crowds; and a robust and anti-intellectual fervor undercuts much discussion among the common folk.

Contrary to much popular opinion, anti-intellectualism in America is of relatively recent vintage, going back to the early 1960s. Before that time, there was general respect for the smart and well-educated, although there were periods in the 1840s and 1850s where the nativists and members of the Know-Nothing Party paraded their "common sense" over "book-learning." However, this had a limited shelf life and was not as peculiarly American as frequently thought.

By 1960-61, the 1950s' era of specialized, post-World War II education, and the development of new professions and industries, led to the development of industry-specific buzz-words and industry jargon that was deliberately used to separate those "in the know" from those mired in ignorance.

Richard Hofstadter's *Anti-Intellectualism in American Life*, a Pulitzer-winning work that exposed the roots and social consequences of American anti-intellectualism, showed that it was the use of arcane means of communication which troubled many people and led to a strong bias against "intellectualism," which was really a resistance to the use of artificially-difficult words designed to create separation between groups in society.

From the period right after World War II, American politics was destined to radically change. Much of this change derived from the heterogenous nature of the armed forces during the War. Farm boys mixed with college grads, and the inherent snobbery of the better-educated soldiers/officers had to take a backseat to the democratized military forces. A lingering resentment on the part of the less-educated soldiers and sailors towards their better-educated counterparts led to a kind of "dumbing-down" of the electorate.

There were those who opportunistically seized the inchoate anti-intellectualism of the American voters. A major example of this type of political carpetbagger was someone who would use his skills and cunning instincts to ascend the political ladder throughout his adult life.

Richard M. Nixon was such a man. Fresh out of the U.S. Navy and burning with political ambition, he hired a Los Angeles attorney and political consultant, Murray M. Chotiner, to run his campaign in 1946 against Jerry Voorhis. Chotiner was a master manipulator and schemer. It was at his political knee that Nixon learned all the dirty tricks that he used against Voorhis, then Helen Gahagan Douglas, and, eventually, against Hubert Humphrey and George McGovern to become the 37th President of the United States.

Chotiner taught Nixon---himself an inherently devious man---the many nuances of political treachery:

- deny that of which you haven't been accused
- engage in underhanded and deceitful tactics, then justify it by appealing to the crowds' fears
- use whatever tactics were necessary to tar the opposing party and candidate
- appeal to the lowest common denominator, realizing that most people are "herd animals," i.e., "The Silent Majority"
- plant evidence on your enemies and/or their supporters
- develop an "enemies' list" and punish those on the list

(Showing that history hasn't changed that much, President Trump manifests much of "Tricky Dick's" worst character defects and personality disorders: he has thin skin; he is easily angered; he suffers from paranoia; he holds the view that "The Media" is his worst enemy; he has a strong desire to attack those attacking him; and, of course, he suffers a conceit about self-importance. The difference between the two men is that Nixon was a competent crook, while Trump is an incompetent reality-TV stumblebum. Yet both appealed to the lowest common denominator in the America electorate).

While American politics has changed little, at its heart, since the time of Andrew Jackson, our legal system did not really start to deteriorate until the time of the **Dred Scott** decision[1]. Generally conceded to be the U.S. Supreme Court's worst decision, **Dred Scott** said that the U.S. Constitution prohibited the Federal judiciary from dealing with the question of slavery in a case brought by a black man. Chief Justice Taney ruled that blacks were not U.S. citizens and, therefore, had no standing to sue. Without standing, the Court lacked power to adjudicate. This case, which prohibited Dred Scott from suing to obtain his freedom, also declared that the Missouri Compromise of 1820 was unconstitutional.

This decision was at least in part responsible for the Civil War, commencing four years later, for it raised sectarian tensions and increased hostilities between North and South.

As bad as that case was, an even worse one was in the offing. Less than 30 years later, the U.S. Supreme Court published a decision that gave corporations the same legal rights as natural human beings under the 14th Amendment to the Constitution. Eventually, the result of that case was the countless uses and abuses of corporate monies to influence and control elections and to dominate the bone and marrow of American political life.

What opened this 'Pandora's Box" was **Santa Clara County v. Southern Pacific Railroad Company**[2], a corporate law decision of the United States Supreme Court on taxation of railroad properties. A headnote issued by the Court Reporter claimed to state the sense of the Court regarding the equal protection clause of the Fourteenth Amendment as it applies to corporations, <u>without the Court having actually made a decision</u> or issued a written opinion on that issue. This was the first time that the Supreme Court was reported to hold that the Fourteenth Amendment's equal protection clause granted constitutional protections to corporations as well as to natural persons, although numerous other cases, since **Dartmouth College v.**

---

[1] *Dred Scott v. Sandford* (1856) 60 U.S. 393

[2] *Santa Clara County v. Southern Pacific Railroad Company* (1886) 118 U.S. 394

***Woodward*[3]** in 1819, had recognized that corporations were entitled to some of the protections of the Constitution.

What was particularly evil about ***Santa Clara County*** is the fact that the "headnote" was not part of the ruling of the Supreme Court and, therefore, could not be technically used as the basis for the claim that corporations were the same as natural persons for 14th Amendment purposes. What is even more sinister is the wholesale legal disregard of the long-held practice that corporations were subject to the statutory limitations of the states in which they were created; corporations were "creatures of statute," and could be created or terminated at the "whim of the legislature." Never was there any jurisprudence in the United States holding that corporations (juridical persons) and human beings (natural persons) should be accorded the same status in the eyes of the law. Then came ***Santa Clara County*** and changed all of that.

From that decision came an entire body of law (Corporate Law) derived from the false notion of equality between juridical and natural persons. A corporation has tax, political, and economic advantages simply unavailable to the average human being, and it was because of this decision that much corruption of our system of politics and laws has arisen.

In short, ***Santa Clara County*** was law created out of whole cloth wherein the Supreme Court allegedly created an equivalency between corporations and natural people for 14th Amendment Equal Protection purposes. However, there was no precedent or other lawful basis for doing so---**and** there was **no holding** in the decision which provided a justification for this so-called equivalency.

Corporate lawyers immediately sprang upon ***Santa Clara County*** as the "precedent" for much legal chicanery that would perpetuate many wrongs against working men, women and children; people of color; immigrants; and other disadvantaged groups, who could not muster the wherewithal to fight corporations in the courts, nor elect officials who might fight for justice through new laws.

---

[3] *Dartmouth College v. Woodward* (1819) 17 U.S. 518

Some 90 years later, in ***Buckley v. Valeo***[4], the U.S. Supreme Court struck down campaign finance reforms from the *Federal Election Campaign Act* of 1971. The Court held that restrictions on campaign spending were unconstitutional, and held that *commercial free speech* was a "right" enjoyed by corporations under the 14th Amendment's Equal Protection Clause.

Showing that the courts are the last bastion of privilege, ***Buckley v. Valeo*** was extended by the U.S. Supreme Court in further cases, including the five to four decisions of ***First National Bank of Boston v. Bellotti***[5] and ***Citizens United v. Federal Election Commission***[6]. The latter held that corporations might spend from their general treasuries during elections, and even foreign-owned/influenced corporations can make campaign contributions in American elections. In 2014, ***McCutcheon v. Federal Election Commission***[7] held that aggregate limits on political giving by an individual are unconstitutional.

Thus, under these holdings, the Supreme Court has made it abundantly clear that corporations and natural human beings are equal in the eyes of the law; that campaign finance reform is merely political puffery; and that we do not live in a system wherein the laws of the land indeed protect democracy.

What are the solutions to these pervasive political problems? The next chapter explores some answers.

---

[4] *Buckley v. Valeo* (1976) 424 U.S. 1
[5] *First National Bank of Boston v. Bellotti* (1978) 435 U.S. 765
[6] *Citizens United v. Federal Election Commission* (2010) 558 U.S. 310
[7] *McCutcheon v. Federal Election Commission* (2014) 134 S.Ct. 1434

CHAPTER 4
WHAT CAN BE DONE TO RIGHT THIS WRONG?

Politics can be defined as the methods of how power is acquired and manifested. Law can be defined as the rules which govern social behavior.

Laws provide the means for rewarding or punishing behavior. Act in a certain way, and you get a benefit; violate a law, and you go to jail (or worse).

For many years, laws were created and existed to protect the monied class: corporations, partnerships, special types of trusts, and high net worth individuals. The interests of ordinary working people; minorities; children; the developmentally disabled; the physically challenged; all were subject to the whims of the big corporations that bought their services; advertised to brainwash them into buying items that brought wealth to business and harmed the rest of us; and created and maintained social, educational, health, financial, and political institutions that kept average and ordinary people enthralled to corporate interests at the expense of their own.

Back in the 1950s, '60s, '70s, and '80s, those of us who were motivated by fighting against injustice typically met in coffee-houses, colleges, neighbors' homes, church or synagogue basements, and formulated action plans, usually involving letter-writing, telephone calls to elected officials, sometimes newspaper ads, and demonstrations (marches and/or sit-ins). The goal was to mobilize public awareness of a wrong and to try to convince the broader public to support those seeking to overcome it.

Some parts of the civil rights, women's rights, anti-war, gay rights, and environmental movements focused on public actions to illustrate the need for concerted public effort to redress our grievances against injustices in the law and/or public attitudes.

However, I also recall attending a number of so-called *liberal* meetings of those in the anti-war, feminist, and environmental movements, and much of their focus was on "educating the public," as if the public was a large but uninformed blob that would do right if it only had enough information. Unfortunately, time has proven that the *intelligentsia* was great at talking, but acting? Not so much. The public, justifiably, felt that the double standard of those who spouted the credo of "do as I say, not as I do" was sufficiently hypocritical to warrant ignoring their clarion calls for action.

During my times in the McCarthy and the McGovern presidential campaigns in 1968 and 1972, we had a number of idealistic liberals who thought that educating people was enough.

We thought that teaching the hungry masses yearning for the right types and amounts of information about the wrongs of the Vietnam War, the dangerous foreign affairs policies of our government, the environmental suicide that we were intent on committing, the racial and gender injustices perpetuated throughout the country, would get them off their couches and into the halls of Congress and/or the White House. Well, it didn't quite work that way, as proved by the successful campaigns of President Richard "Tricky Dick" Nixon in 1968 and 1972. In short, the educate-everybody-and-they'll-be-good-citizens brigades limited themselves into social fecklessness.

Today, we live, arguably, in a "TMI" (Too Much Information) age, one where we are constantly bombarded with, and distracted by, inputs from TV, radio, print media, social media, and water-cooler gossip. When you couple the TMI affliction with the decreased ability to critically think due to today's inferior educational systems, many people want to "do something," but lack guidance on what steps can be taken to fight wrongs.

There are a number of things that can be done. We live in a different environment these days; the world is more connected than ever; though the Internet information is widely shared on an unprecedented scale; and there is a generational divide that prevents old-fashioned ideas that are harmful to many from being universally adopted and accepted as "Gospel truth."

The Millennials and post-Millennials may be aggravating to those of us who learned to read and think and perceive the world in linear fashion---they most assuredly do not---but they have the power to acquire and synthesize more information more rapidly than any preceding generation. They are suffering from crippling student debt, the inability to find meaningful and stable employment, a housing market which is a joke, and a lack of health care. They have real problems that dwarf those of past generations.

Moreover, they have ideas and values which, although sometimes poorly-articulated, give rise to the hope that a new generation with new thinking about how people should interact will lead us from our present darkness into a world of light, learning, and love for one another, a world not based on greed but on sharing, not based on ambition but on aspiration for creating a rising tide that lifts all boats, not based on "win-lose" but on social, economic, and political justice that creates true equal opportunities and incentives to be the best possible people.

Step 1: Know Who You are (the Size of Your Hat)

Each person gets to wear the size of "hat" that fits, i.e., the dimension of one's concern for living in society, and how to give back to the people who bore you, raised you, educated you, and gave you your start in this world.

Some people are inherently parochial and private. They have an attitude of "I've got mine; to hell with you, Jack." These are not people who will reach out to help a neighbor build a new home, put out a fire, clean up a community, or otherwise volunteer to make this a better town. They wear very small hats.

A few in this category---those with more education and cultural awareness---try to make excuses for their noninvolvement in volunteer activity by saying "Well, I make my contribution through my job. I'm a doctor/lawyer/police officer, etc., after all."

B.S. Your job is how you *make a living*; what you do as a volunteer, the level of sacrifice you make for the community, is how you *make a life*. There's a huge difference there, and don't let sophistical arguments persuade you otherwise.

Some people are a little more externally oriented. They belong to a church, a temple, a mosque; they volunteer with the Boy Scouts or Girl Scouts; they help with neighborhood clean-ups; they belong to volunteer organizations that try to improve civic life in some respects, whether through schools, hospitals, libraries, or other groups that reach out to improve the community.

They may feel good about their activities (as they should), but they are still fairly private and completely local. Their hats are a little larger, but not by much, since they are still busy taking care of their own and are not interested in extending their reach beyond their own block or neighborhood.

Others, a much smaller group, recognize how connected we are, and they offer help not only locally but across multiple communities. They may be involved with structural changes in how the police departments run; in making improvements in the educational system; in focusing on refinements in the delivery of health care; or helping veterans, assisting the homeless, or working on the environment. These folks wear much bigger hats. They are making genuine sacrifices for the extended community's good.

The smallest group consists of people who see the big picture and are willing to make sacrifices for the sake of a movement: anti-war; pro-Civil Rights; feminist; pro-environment. These are people who live and breathe for a cause. Dr. King; Cesar Chavez; Mahatma Gandhi; Victoria Woodhull; Susan B. Anthony; all led with a big vision for a better world, and with the dedication to that cause, no matter what.

The first and fourth groups, the "no-vision" and the "world vision" people, live at opposite poles. The first, composed of highly-selfish people, does not see how self-limiting they are. They do not understand how they are cutting off the possibility of self-fulfillment by doing something outside of their own private interests that will improve the community in which they live. By contrast, the fourth is made up of people who have in most instances given up on the joys of family life, personal accomplishment, and having a rich social life. Instead, they are so focused on working to solve macro-problems that individual concerns are of little to no importance to them

Both extremes can be hazardous to the psychological and spiritual health of their members. Pure selfishness leads to a fundamentally barren and pointless life, one without true meaning or fulfillment. Conversely, living a "saintly" life without any personal time or sense of personal rewards can be equally barren. People who live for a cause may derive great spiritual fulfillment from living a highly elevated life, but what they gain there is too often lost by missing a healthy family or social life.

However, there is one fundamental benefit to being a member of the fourth group. Once enough people join the cause, then it is a mutually-reinforcing movement, with a sense of collective purpose, fulfillment, and broad meaning. Then, the camaraderie of being "brothers and sisters in the trenches" supersedes the notion of going out and having beers on the weekend. Being "warriors" in the sense of "fighting the good fight" in a community of like-minded people is an immensely satisfying experience. Those of us who fought against the Vietnam War; who fought for Civil Rights; for the Women's Movement; for the environment; all came away feeling that they did their best to make this a better society, a better world.

Indeed, the motivation to living this type of life is at the core of the 1906 speech given to Stanford University students, "The Moral Equivalent of War," by the great American psychologist, William James. In it, James points out how Mankind is intrinsically warlike, and craves the attributes of war: discipline; self-sacrifice for the sake of a Noble Cause; the call to glory; the betterment of one's Nation-State. We all have a choice: pursue the "glories of war," or participate in the "moral equivalent" of war by engaging in activities that embody those more noble aspects of human life: altruism; empathy; self-sacrifice in favor of the needs of a meaningful cause; a burning desire to make this a more just, constructive, and verdant world. One method of life is oriented towards destruction and death; the other, the creation of a world where the possibilities of human growth are endless.

We all have choices in what we do. So, before deciding what you want to do, you must first decide who you are: what size hat do you want to wear, and what is the extent to which you want to work to improve your neighborhood, your community, your state, your nation, your world.

Step 2: Know What You Want (and Keep it Real)

One of the problems seen in so-called liberal or progressive groups is the egoistic fixation on their cause, to the exclusion of others. It has gotten down to absurd distinctions: <u>this</u> group is about saving the dolphins, while <u>that</u> group is about saving the whales. Then, the members get into ridiculous arguments about which group is "better." It devolves into stupidly self-righteous arguments about who is doing more for the environment. ***Really?!***

The conservative members of society may also do lots of good things: volunteering in schools, Scouting, 4H Clubs, hospitals, providing day-care services, providing veteran outreach, helping the homeless, working for animal-care, looking in on elderly shut-ins, among many choices.

Meanwhile, the right-wing corporate troglodytes don't care about any part of the environment, or civil rights, or immigration as a moral issue; they're just interested in making as much money as possible.

The point is, there are so many options from which to choose that a good-hearted person cannot truly say "There's nothing for me to do."

If you have no idea where you'd like to volunteer, here's a suggestion: over a 12-month period join anywhere from three to six groups. See what most appeals to you, based on your existing interests, skills (or the skills you'd like to develop), and what you feel would be a good fit for you. Once you have a good idea of what you'd like to do, then select a group where you can add your talents to what everyone else is doing, and help to advance their cause. You'd be surprised how good you feel, working in a community of like-minded people.

Step 3: Get a Road Map (and Don't Be Afraid to Make Course Corrections)

We are a much more polarized society than we used to be. Religious beliefs; identity politics; narrowly-defined agendas; and all the cultural baggage that goes with these groups, make it difficult for us to find common ground.

We used to share the experience of having fought together during World War II against common enemies who threatened our way of life. Coming from that background, members of Congress and state legislatures were much more united and bi-partisan than at any time since then. We will probably never have that type of massive, shared experience again, fighting against a common foe.

(Because we seem to do better when we join forces in opposing a major enemy, it's probably best to find ways to identify common foes that can unite us. One such way is to find citizens' action groups with such a focus.) One such group is called "The Asteroids Club," http://asteroidsclub.org. Their Welcome says:

"The Asteroids Club is a new approach to communicating about the civic problems that polarize - and paralyze - us. The concept grew out of the field of moral psychology, which tells us that people are more likely to find common ground when they unite to fight common threats. We hope you will join in our adventure and help us grow this new idea by starting an Asteroids Club in your hometown. There are so many asteroids and so little time."

The antithesis of bi-partisanship is hyper-partisanship, a political malady that now affects all of us. However, there are many things that we can to do to dramatically reduce the tensions that divide us into such a disparate society. The following actions can be taken, starting at the local, i.e., county, level with efforts to get statewide, and eventually national, legislation to make these changes permanent.

a. Elect Fewer Hyper-Partisans, e.g., Have More Open Primaries

Hyper-partisans derive support from political parties for two main reasons. First, strong positions tend to distinguish one side (party affiliation) from the other, thus increasing name recognition. Second, strong positions make it easier to raise campaign funds from core party members and wealthy donors. This is the direct result of the use of private money to fund public functions, i.e., political campaigns and elections.

It is inappropriate in a truly democratic setting to have a false equivalency between corporate interests and those of natural human beings, but it is precisely because of this equivalency---sanctioned by the courts since 1886---that we have to beg for money from well-to-do donors, all of whom have their own agendas to promote. This situation is not conducive to the exercise of truly democratic principles or the achievement of more humane, justice-oriented laws.

Hyper-partisanship dramatically reduces the changes for bi-partisan work in all legislative contexts. Any side that is seen to compromise with the other is deemed by the party leadership as craven or traitorous to "key party principles." The problem with this approach is that there is a huge disconnect between the interests of political parties and the constituents they purport to represent.

There are many advantages to open primaries. These are some of the biggest ones, according to the *Open Primaries: Pro vs. Con* study conducted by the League of Women Voters of Oak Ridge (March 1, 2012).

1. Open primaries favor individual choices over party choices. (There are some things about which we may agree with a political party, but the days of strong identification and affiliation with the party's "brand" are long gone.)

2. Open primaries advance the two most-favored candidates to the general election. (Again, this is a reflection of individuals' choices, rather than "Democrat versus Republican" affiliations.)

3. Open primaries produce competitive, substantive general elections. (This is where real differences in issues arise; this is where

there can be a genuine "competition of ideas" between candidates; and this is where people will get to see that they have greater choices than in the Democratic Party versus Republican Party horse-race.)

4. Open primaries provide greater access to independents/third-party candidates. (Since the base of independent voters has been growing over the years, open primaries will allow more independent candidates to seek office and bring their ideas before the public.)

5. Open primaries lessen the importance of party affiliation and reduce the vestiges of patronage that have afflicted American politics since 1830. (Because of the frustrations with party politics, fewer people on both liberal and conservative parts of our political spectrum feel strongly about their membership in a party. This is especially so among the younger voters.)

6. Open primaries require more from voters in assessing candidates and evaluating their positions on issues. (Open primaries, by definition, will tend to deemphasize personalities and will increase the importance of issues. However, this will require voters to be more aware of the news, to be more informed about what is important as opposed to concentrating on salacious details of the candidates' personal lives.)

7. Open primaries will promote civility and emphasize what is of importance to the voters rather than wasting time and money on the candidates bashing each other.

Indeed, in many polls and focus-group studies, voters have expressed increasing frustration, disappointment, and an unwillingness to participate in politics because of its lack of civility, mutual respect, and failure to address issues. Instead of "slinging mud," voters want candidates to talk about the problems that concern voters and discuss possible solutions that make sense to people in the community, the state, and/or the nation.

Some criticize open primaries because, they argue, "bland politics" will arise from this type of voting system. There are claims that open primaries will attract more moderate candidates and that party affiliations will fall by the wayside.

Precisely. That's **exactly** what is needed.

For years, voters have complained about gridlock, not only in Washington, D.C., but also in their statehouses. They have noted that the Democrats attack the Republicans, and vice versa. They see that instead of people reaching across the aisle, their politicians cluster together and develop sound-bites that describe why "the other side" is full of bad guys who don't have the citizens' interests at heart.

This exercise may give the sound-bite authors a sense of moral authority, but it does absolutely nothing to advance the legislative agenda that would serve the country's or the state's needs.

As we have seen over the last quarter century, there has been an increasing division in our elective processes, so much so that we have even adopted a new verb: to *primary* a candidate, i.e., to mount a campaign in the primary election against an incumbent who wasn't strong enough in supporting, or who opposed, a party's position. The 2004 and 2008 elections, in particular, saw the Tea Party's faction within the Republican Party going after people such as Sen. Dick Lugar of Indiana through this process; and many other incumbents also faced the possibility of being primaried in subsequent elections.

A number of Republicans (and a few Democrats) have resigned in 2018, given the conditions in Congress and how frustrating it is to run for their constituents, only to find that in order to stay in office, they have to violate their voters' needs or ignore their concerns, in order to preserve party unity.

It is this internal conflict between what it took to get into and what it takes to stay in office that prompts many otherwise fine senators or representatives to say "enough" and to head for the exits. We have seen how Congress could not even come to terms with the annual budget, but had to provide government funding through the use of five Continuing Resolutions during the first 14 months of President Donald J. Trump's presidency. If Congress can't figure out how to come up with a budget, how can they be expected to proceed with new and urgently-needed legislation on all the pending measures that have been placed in abeyance since Trump took office?

In reality, political parties have long outlived their usefulness. In the past, they were used to unite people who shared a majority of beliefs, who valued the agendas argued by their party, and used the party for certain types of patronage.

Nowadays, with divergent beliefs everywhere, it is frustrating to look for leadership when most people have differing views on topics ranging from abortion to climate change to taxes to health care to education to immigration to family values.

Additionally, parties do not necessarily obtain facts that can be discussed objectively. Instead, they marshal arguments that can be used to denigrate their opponents and win positions of power. The interests of common people? They're given lip service, but seldom, if ever, carry weight when it comes to elections or afterwards.

Indeed, according to a recent report from ConnectUSfund.org, political parties have more demerits than strengths: drowning individual "voices," removing progressive ideals from the party's platform, espousing increasingly partisan approaches instead of taking the bipartisan tack, false education ("our party's great, yours is terrible" based on half-truths and outright lies), and an overemphasis on raising money and acquiring power rather than on constructing programs that can garner widespread bipartisan support.

Because of our fixation on entertainment, we supposedly love the strong partisan battles. Editors of TV shows, newspapers, blogs, magazines, and radio programs think that we are addicted to political brawls. Perhaps for the moment of excitement, yes. But when it comes to being truly devoted to the political process and to the politicians that drive it, not so much. However, the editors gear their stories to what they believe "sells." That includes appeals to the lowest common denominator, and that explains why we have seen an explosion in reality TV shows.

The dual love-hate relationship we have with politics and politicians is based on the excitement a junkie feels when he's about to get a hit of his favorite drug, and the hatred he feels for being enslaved by it.

The more extreme and partisan our politics is, the more of a love-hate feeling we have for it.

The solution is that we have to return to the "bland" type of politics where we actually recognize that we have more in common than we realize; that we have real problems that the other side may see more clearly than we do; and that we need to work together to solve these problems, in good faith, and with civil discussions of what can work best to achieve our goals, along with heartfelt commitments to stay loyal to what benefits the community as a whole, instead of promoting the interests of the privileged class.

Four Areas of Concern for Liberals and Conservatives

There are common areas of concern for liberals, and common areas of concern for conservatives.

The Liberals
- **Climate change** – generally deemed to be the Number One threat to our existence.

- **Inequalities** – especially with the Millennials, who were raised in an atmosphere of equality in all things, this is deeply troubling on a visceral level. Racism, gender bias, and hostility towards members of the LGBTQ community raise their hackles like nothing else. And the popularity of Bernie Sanders and Elizabeth Warren have raised progressives' anger about income inequality to levels not seen since the Great Depression, nearly 90 years ago.

The Conservatives
- **Entitlements** – they view these as unfair programs to give special privileges to selected groups. For the conservatives, they believe that these are economically untenable.
- **The Breakdown of the Family Unit and Family Values** – they view the dramatic reductions in the number of marriages, the fact that fewer children are being born, and that many children are born out of wedlock, with the threats to the quality of life from which these kids suffer.

Liberals are shocked that conservatives don't agree with the existence of climate change. They ask, "How can you deny science? How can you reject facts? Don't you understand that this could accelerate the 6th Mass Extinction, and that we're in the middle of it?"

Liberals don't understand the conservatives' views about inequality. Racism has been a major part of this country's history for hundreds of years, but race isn't the only barrier between people. Gender, sexual orientation, religion, handicapped status, and the big one, <u>income</u>, divide us as never before. Yet conservatives don't see inequality as a huge problem.

On the other hand, conservatives feel that our so-called "entitlement" programs are a prescription for economic disaster. They look at Social Security (not actually an "entitlement," but an "earned benefit"); Medicare/Medicaid; and other government programs that provide financial assistance to families in distress, and they say "Who's going to pay for all this? We don't have or soon won't have the money for these programs."

Likewise, the conservatives lament the seeming lack of concern by liberals for family values. This is actually not true, but the problem is that the conservatives' expressions of support for family values have frequently been used as a way of suppressing women, restricting choices, and preventing more than half the population from living lives based on personal dignity, respect, and autonomy.

What the conservatives fail to understand is that their values are often stratified in a patriarchal manner that restricts instead of empowers. With advances in medicine, including the invention of the birth control pill, women have more choices than ever before. Yet, many of them have gone overboard and now don't want to get married and have families until much later, or never, perhaps not realizing just how important the family unit is.

While homosexuality is certainly more visible than ever, and people who are homosexual should never be suppressed because of their orientation, the fact is that heterosexuality is the overwhelmingly dominant sexual motif and there are many who feel that there is too much emphasis on the LGBTQ culture in today's society.

In the face of pressures from homosexuals to adopt and raise children, it should be noted that there is a major study, undertaken by Cornell University in 2009, which shows that children raised in a two-parent, male-female home with healthy values and good communications grow up to have far fewer problems with the law, with education, with health and life expectancy, and with relationships. Conversely, children who grow up in single-parent homes are faced with an avalanche of problems with the law; risk-taking behaviors; alcohol/drug abuse; education; income; health; and relationships.

However, it may also be profoundly true that a child raised in a two-parent home, regardless of the parents' gender, full of love, trust, and good communications will nonetheless thrive better than a child in a single-parent home.

Because liberals want to be seen as progressive, tolerant, and non-judgmental, they don't use the language of traditional family advocates. They don't put a line in the sand and say "We stand on the side of the family with male and female parents, where they emphasize stability, good values, and good communications." Liberals shrink from using language that espouses these traditional values, because to be heard doing so may make others think that they aren't progressive, liberal, and in favor of freedom.

Liberals often forget the importance of having a male and a female role-model in the home: the father to impose loving discipline and to help the children grow into well-behaved adults who respect themselves and respect others, and the mother to provide emotional and psychological support and a sense of belonging.

What conservatives fail to see is that the biggest threats to the family and to family values are economic. The lack of jobs, especially for minorities, puts pressure on couples to wait much longer than they used to. The costs of raising children these days is astronomical. The price of health care, education, and all the other things needed to provide a safety net for kids is sky-high, and there is no relief in sight.

Because both sides feel that the world is closing in on them, they take increasingly-rigid positions on these issues. And, because of the structure of our political system, many politicians are opportunistic, catering to those whose beliefs are cast in concrete.

Politicians who take extreme, hyper-partisan positions on either end of the ideological spectrum do not dare take the time to start working with their political opponents. Yet, it is because of how deep our problems are that we need to avoid hyper-partisanship more than ever. It is vital that we learn how to work together once again, to fight common enemies and to figure out ways to make this a better world.

There are many more than just these four "asteroids" that are threats to us. But as a place to start, these four topics---climate change; inequality; entitlements; and family values---all have major impacts on our lives. All four are areas where we could profitably start working together to solve problems that have the ability to wipe us out if left unchecked.

And if we don't, then God help us.

b. Weaken Pressures to Act Hyper-Partisan, e.g., Counteract the *Citizens United* Ruling by Taking Private Money Out of Politics

How do we reduce, if not eliminate, the pressures for hyper-partisanship in our political processes?

Political parties have been fundraising machines for many years. Hyper-partisanship is the chief selling tool for them. There are many financial contributors to parties as opposed to the individual candidates. Part of this is legally-based, but part of it derives from the notion that parties know best how to allocate funds in ways that advance the donors' interests.

Money is the source of problems in our political (and legal) systems. Politically speaking, ever since ***Buckley v. Vallejo***, courts have repeatedly held that campaign financing by corporations was just fine; that limits on campaign spending were infringements on corporations' Free Speech rights; and that laws restricting corporations' "rights" to contribute were unconstitutional.

No case more strongly espoused this last judicial principle than ***Citizens United***. There, the U.S. Supreme Court, in a tight, 5-4 decision, said that corporations would be given *carte blanche* when it came to campaign spending. Under **Citizens United**, "Super PACs" (Political Action Committees) were created and became shadow political parties that would collect huge amounts of money from various high net worth individuals and corporations, and spend it to advance their pro-rich agendas.

The law, in its majestic equality, forbids rich and poor alike to sleep under bridges, to beg in the streets, and to steal their bread. - Anatole France

---

Would a presidential campaign, a la Bernie Sanders' in 2016, or moves towards a constitutional amendment have the effect and immediate payoff that **Citizens United** had? Almost assuredly not.

One of the serious side notes from the #Me Too movement is the fact that women (usually younger ones) perform most of the campaign funding solicitations. The donors---usually older, white, and well-heeled men---frequently have a sense of sexual entitlement and often have no compunction about speaking and/or acting in ways that threaten the women's personal integrity and sense of safety. (*Political Fundraisers Face Harassment From An Endless Stream Of Men With Money*, Molly Redden, HuffingtonPost.com, June 16, 2018.)

Changes in major social beliefs take place over time, and it is changes in those beliefs which seed the ground for legal changes.

The solution, it seems clear, is to take private money out of public functions, i.e., political campaigns, lobbying; and anything to do with the creation or modification of laws. **Only when public money is used for public purposes does our democracy have a chance at fulfilling its potential.**

But how do progressives convert "Democracy's promise" to "promises kept?" Isn't the principle that "money is the mother's milk of politics" so deeply ingrained in our system that there is no way to effect structural changes? Not necessarily. Perhaps we can learn the lessons taught by the conservatives over the last couple of generations to bring about deep-seated, systemic change.

The Conservative Rebellion

The Republicans have, for the last 45-50 years, been busy at the local level, developing their constituencies to support candidates for school boards; city councils; city government; and county government. Then, with control of the city and county governments, along with their corresponding party apparatus, these candidates went on to state government: the Senate; the Assembly; the Governorship.

Through interstate actions, a political movement began to counteract that of the liberals' efforts in the 1960s. The so-called "Silent Majority," consisting of "Boll Weevil" Democrats and suburban Republicans, espoused economically and socially conservative positions, and continued the trends of center-right politics, concentrating on local action.

The liberals, by contrast, had a broader, nationwide pattern of activity: street marches; sit-ins; media campaigns. However, on the local level, the liberals failed to focus. The liberals, especially the so-called New Left, have been unable to organize a coffee klatch, much less a revolution, because of their lack of discipline and unwillingness to focus on group objectives.

What we saw over the period from 1968 to 1994 was a conservative rebellion against the anti-war, civil rights, free speech, feminist, and gay pride movements geared towards peace and greater inclusiveness in society. The so-called "White Flight" to the suburbs, to escape urbanization (read: an increase in minority populations in the cities), led to a two-tier education system and structure of family life.

Those in the suburbs (almost all white) had higher incomes, better schools, and an overall better quality of life. Those living in the inner cities (almost all black and/or brown) faced a daily struggle against economic hardship; racial Balkanization; poor quality schools; higher *per capita* costs of living; difficulties with law enforcement; and a degraded quality of life.

During the 1994 mid-term elections, the Republicans, led by Newt Gingrich and Dick Armey, took many policy ideas from a conservative think tank, *The Heritage Foundation*, and pledged to work on specific pieces of legislation. This policy platform, called the "Contract With America," articulated the action items the Republicans planned to pursue should they become the majority party in the House of Representatives for the first time since 1954.

Once the mid-term elections were over in 1994, the Republicans had gained 54 seats in the House of Representatives and nine seats in the Senate. Conservatives viewed their electoral success as proof that their conservative rebellion was winning, and that they represented a new trend in American politics: smaller government ("so small, you could drown it in a bathtub"); lower taxes; more entrepreneurial activity; and tort and welfare reform.

With the new conservative majority in the House of Representatives, President Bill Clinton was forced to cut back on his liberal campaign promises. He advanced welfare-to-work legislation, straight out of the Republicans' playbook, that imposed stringent limitations on the right to get welfare, and that promised to punish "generations of welfare chiselers" who had allegedly been bilking the taxpayers out of untold amounts of money. Likewise, anti-lawyer legislation in the name of "tort reform" was passed both federally and on the state level, making it much harder for tort plaintiffs to use the courts to get justice in the face of corporate malfeasance.

Meanwhile, throughout the 1990s, liberal leadership in Congress was feckless. Lacking discipline, coherent strategies, and bold leadership, the Democrats were considered to be the party of losers. Ruining their reputation as progressives, Democrats were saddled with Bill Clinton's sexual dalliances with Monica Lewinsky. They were constantly having to battle back, always on the defensive, and never able to advance liberal programs.

Even worse, the 2000 Presidential election was tainted with the electoral fraud of the ultra-right-wing supporters of George W. Bush. In November 2000, although he won a significant majority of the popular vote, former Vice President Al Gore lost the election by electoral college votes. There were scandals in several states, but by far the worst case was in Florida. Some said that Gore was "hung by 'hanging chads'."

Will the Millennials Save Us? How About Gen Z?

During the last 24 years since the "Contract With America," we have seen even more extreme political elements come to the fore: evangelicals and the Christian right led to Tea Party members who were followed by even more conservative evangelicals ("End Timers"), who were followed by neo-Nazis and alt-right advocates. Not content with merely espousing crazy ideas, the extreme right-wingers put themselves into the streets, frequently serving as counter-demonstrators whenever there was a liberal/progressive march or protest, especially in the wake of the increasing number of black people killed by police around the country. Many of the strongest right-wing sentiments came from evangelical churches throughout the South.

However, Millennials from the right have been leaving their religious affiliations in record numbers, due to their perceptions that the Christian right is full of hypocrisy, judgment, and hatred of LGBTQ people. (Cox, Daniel, (2018-01-24). "Are White Evangelicals Sacrificing the Future in Search of the Past?" FiveThirtyEight.com).

We certainly cannot place all our hopes on the Millennials coming to the rescue, but there is clearly a generational divide that shows Millennials and their successors as being far more tolerant, open to a variety of sexual relationships, and less judgmental than their predecessors. There is a phrase widely uttered by Millennials: "Don't judge me." The etiology of the phrase seems to be their reaction to the rigorous life-style expectations of the elder clergy and their elder supporters. The youngsters simply were having none of it, and their own rebellion led to self-exile in large numbers from the conventional churches as well as the evangelical ones.

With large numbers of young people leaving traditional religious practices and the Republican Party, is their exodus a harbinger of new affiliations? Perhaps. What seems reasonably clear at this point is that they are not content to sit in Daddy's easy-chair and watch the world go by.

Millennials have rightly been called a generation of <u>snowflakes</u>; of self-entitled little wimps and wusses who love whining and complaining about how hard life is; and how they need participation trophies to soothe their feelings.

I'm a Baby Boomer, and proud of it in many ways. I'm proud of the anti-war, pro-Civil- and Women's-Rights movements. I'm proud of our generally more tolerant views in many areas of life.

But I'm also deeply ashamed of many Boomers, who transferred a collective mentality into an individualistic *ethos* and who had to "feel" everything, since they didn't have the discipline to stick to the hard sciences and make choices that would benefit generations to come.

As a huge demographic, the Boomers had the first opportunity to jump start our society into one based on equality, peace, and economic justice, but that would have required making sacrifices, and the Boomers, by and large, were highly averse to making personal sacrifices. They made the immoral decision to be amoral in the face of many challenges. They bought into the "Me Generation" B.S. of the 1970s and viewed society as a gigantic piggybank from which they could extract whatever they wanted. They forgot the vital Law of Balance: you must put back what you take out, or you'll drain your account.

As a result, they bought into the Ronald Reagan B.S. of the 1980 Presidential campaign and followed the pipe-dream of "trickle-down" economics, which was objectively ridiculous the moment it came out of the mouth of Arthur Laffer and his economic cronies. They wanted to believe in "voodoo economics" (thank you, George H.W. Bush, for that wonderful phrase) because it promised that they would get more out than they put in, every child's fantasy. However, so many failed to make the follow-up analysis to see that writing "rubber checks" on the government's accounts would eventually lead to disaster (which it did).

The Boomers chose to live lives of self-deception, and they adopted the political platitudes of the right-wing pundits on radio and television, as well as those running for Congress. Notwithstanding the

Women's Movement of the 1960s and '70s, many Boomer men grew up with a moral double-standard when it came to dealing with women: give lip service to them in public, but behind closed doors treat them like sexual toys to be played with at will. Hence, the shameful conduct of Harvey Weinstein and those of his ilk over the years, starting in the 1970s and going forward.

The Gen X cohort was/is too small to make a significant impact on society, although many of them manifested many of the worst qualities of the Baby Boomers, along with pre-Millennial traits of excessive sensitivity and impatience. Because of their small size, I'll largely ignore them here.

While Millennials have been studied *ad infinitum*, their demographic successor, Generation Z, seems to be the real deal in terms of wanting to make this a better world. Smarter, more savvy in a lot of ways, Gen Z kids were born right before 2000, and they have grown up in chaos, politically and financially. They want to save the world.

Yes.

They want to save the world.

They are tech-smart; operate in a world of "group-think" but are inherently suspicious of propaganda; want to make real changes in how people live; are open to new ideas, especially those coming from the tech/digital world; and believe in freedom.

Unlike the Millennials, who were a selfish, self-regarding ("Let me take a Selfie") generation, Gen Z favors making this a better world. Their hero is Malala Yousafzai, the youthful Pakistani education campaigner, who was shot in the face by the Taliban, and is the youngest ever Nobel Prize recipient.

Gen Z youngsters have organized many progressive activities that harken back to the days of the 1960s when we were protesting the Vietnam War; campaigning for civil rights; working for feminist goals; seeking to make this a better society. Many of the same tactics we used are now being followed, albeit in a high-tech mode, by Gen Z.

Will Gen Z lead to a better political system? Possibly. If they listen and synthesize, then share, they have the potential to be much wiser than their Gen X and Baby Boomer grandparents. The question is whether they will learn from the mistakes of the past. (But that has *always* been the question, hasn't it?)

Many of them are smart as whips. They get the sad reality that theirs is the first generation that objectively has less going for it than prior generations. Born into a world of political and financial turmoil, many of them have studied, but cannot viscerally understand, what it's like to have grown up in a pre-9/11 world. They have no sense of loss of the freedoms that we enjoyed as a routine part of life. They simply know what they know, and many of them have figured out how to beat the system, not for greed, but as a matter of convenience. Incredibly bright, quite a few of them simply have no patience for the bottlenecks put in their way by society's gatekeepers. So they figured out ways around them.

The Millennials and especially the Gen Z cohorts who have studied the right things realize that structural change is the name of the game. Not only do we have to move towards Open Primaries, but we also have to change the socio-political and legal environment to make it possible to get rid of the influence of **Citizens United**. They understand that this is about curtailing the influence of political parties, and about money, which is what **Citizens United** is all about.

People in this group are used to crowd-funding, so they are completely familiar with the idea of using public money for matters of public good, such as elections. Why should the Koch brothers, or Sheldon Adelson, or Robert Mercer, or many other conservative (or worse) plutocrats be allowed to buy elections? The answer is, they shouldn't.

Gen Z understands this and is already starting to fight against the influence of private money to fund public functions. It will take time; it will take discipline of the sort displayed by the Republicans in the 1970s through today; but, unlike the Baby Boomers who were ill-disciplined, today's youth understands that they really have a big mandate to follow, and they won't have a second chance.

A lot of them are on it already. Continue to watch for the "Blue Tide" for years to come.

c. Rebuild Cross-Party Relationships, e.g., Change the Legislative Calendar to 3 Weeks On, 1 Week Off

Due to Congressional rescheduling and calendar adjustments, members of Congress get to work on Tuesday mornings and leave for home on Thursday afternoons. This kind of work schedule means that they are no longer career politicians, but are political braceros.

What was a common schedule for generations was that Senators and Congresspeople would work five days a week for three weeks in a row, then would take off for a week to return to their families and their Districts. During each three week period, members of each house would invariably spend time with each other, over drinks and/or dinner. They would cultivate relationships. This applied even on a cross-party basis. It would not be unusual for Republicans to dine with Democrats, and maybe attend a baseball or football game with them.

This practice built relationships, even friendships. With those friendships, it was virtually unheard of for Congresspeople or Senators to utter the type of vitriol and hyperbole that is commonly expressed these days in both houses. This type of collegiality was conducive to compromise and getting things done that would benefit many people as opposed to splintered groups within a constituency.

Relationship-building is vital. People will quit a party; people will quit a seat; but it's much harder to convince them to quit a good relationship that has produced benefits for many people.

Imagine a Congress filled with people who are the products of open primaries; whose campaigns were paid for with public funds; and who had to work three weeks on, one week off.

This would be a Congress filled with serious people, devoted to serving their constituencies and the public as a whole, who were dedicated to making this a much better country and state.

This would be a Congress where the interests of ordinary people would receive top priority; where the wants of high net worth individuals and corporations would be subordinate to the needs of the common man and woman; where people would have a true champion to represent their interests instead of pursuing wealthy people's agendas.

This would be a Congress where we would no longer accede to the wishes of a narcissist-in-chief, but would exercise the legislative power as an expression of the will of the People.

It would be a national legislature that could and would follow the paths of conscience, in helping our country return to its historical goals and dreams. It would be a law-making body which would be under the guidance of men and women devoted to building our leadership in the world through the exercise of truly democratic traditions and practices.

Imagine, then, a Congress (and its counterpart in all 50 states) where the People were able to get help with education; health; taxes; infrastructure; moving from a fossil-fuel based to a renewable-energy economy; where we devoted significant money to R & D to help improve our knowledge base; where we provided training to upgrade working people's skills; where we provided people with opportunities to serve their country in so many ways; where we would develop a legal system and police system that got rid of institutionalized jailing of minorities; where we developed programs of foreign aid and cultural support around the world; where we supported arts and the humanities; where we reduced (or, better, eliminated) our addiction to military spending ("welfare for the military-industrial complex"); and where, above all else, we dedicated ourselves to the proposition that Americans are a remarkable people. Just give us a chance to show it.

CHAPTER 5
AMEND THE 14TH AMENDMENT

We need to amend the 14th Amendment to the U.S. Constitution to insert the word "natural" immediately before each instance of the word "person." That would do away with the pernicious doctrine that "a corporation is a person" for Equal Protection purposes, and it would allow states to restrict "commercial free speech," which means that billionaires like the Koch brothers could no longer buy elections and politicians.

Plutocrats already have enough power; they should not be able to buy political power, too. The Gen Z contingent is beginning to make its moves already. For example, strong anti-gun sentiment is being mustered nationally as the direct result of the Marjory Stoneman Douglas High School students from Parkland, Florida making trips to their state legislature in Tallahassee, as well as Congress. They have led marches, protest rallies, and developed social media campaigns and are the shock troops of a new political movement to stop gun violence.

The old monied class may temporarily be in the catbird seat, but the students of today will start to assume leadership positions within the next five years. I strongly suspect that they will not allow the Top 1% to continue to dominate the American body politic much longer; too much is at stake to allow this tragic pattern to continue.

Despite what was said earlier---changes in major social beliefs take place over time, and it is changes in those beliefs which seed the ground for legal changes---there are some parts of our social structure which can suddenly shift. For example, the move to legalize gay marriage took place fairly quickly. Likewise, the #MeToo movement exploded, starting in the autumn of 2017. Now, entire industries have been rocked by the call for treating women with dignity, respect, and equality.

The need to reduce hyper-partisanship is vital as part of efforts to make politics more useful. However, we need legal reforms to make sure that these changes become a permanent part of the political landscape.

Thus, we need laws that will provide for open primaries; that will institute public campaign financing; and that will remove the power of corporations to be treated the same as natural persons.

It is the desire to rid us of private financing of public campaigns, and of the false equivalency between corporations and human beings that is the essential basis for eliminating the ***Citizens United*** ruling. If we don't act soon to delete this insidious influence on the American body politic, our society will be doomed to a dystopian future where we all must pledge allegiance to our corporate masters and forsake our basic humanity.

How do we change or correct an amendment to the Constitution?

It's not easy.

The procedure is spelled out in Article V of the U.S. Constitution. Either a two-thirds vote in both the House of Representatives and the Senate must support a proposed change, or there must be a constitutional convention called for by a two-thirds majority of the 50 states, i.e., 34 of the 50 must so vote. Interestingly, of the 27 amendments to the Constitution, *none* have come about because of holding a constitutional convention.

According to the Office of the Federal Register ("OFR"), Congress proposes an amendment in the form of a joint resolution. Since the President does not have a constitutional role in the amendment process, the joint resolution does not go to the White House for signature or approval. The original document is forwarded directly to the National Archives and Records Administration for processing and publication. The OFR adds legislative history notes to the joint resolution and publishes it in slip law format. The OFR also assembles an information package for the States which includes formal "redline" copies of the joint resolution, copies of the joint resolution in slip law format, and the statutory procedure for ratification under 1 U.S.C. 106b.

The Archivist submits the proposed amendment to the States for their consideration by sending a letter of notification to each Governor along with the informational material prepared by the OFR. The Governors then formally submit the amendment to their State legislatures, or the state calls for a convention, depending on what Congress has specified. In the past, some State legislatures have not waited to receive official notice before taking action on a proposed amendment. When a State ratifies a proposed amendment, it sends the Archivist an original or certified copy of the State action, which is immediately conveyed to the Director of the Federal Register. The OFR examines ratification documents for facial legal sufficiency and an authenticating signature. If the documents are found to be in good order, the Director acknowledges receipt and maintains custody of them. The OFR retains these documents until an amendment is adopted or fails, and then transfers the records to the National Archives for preservation.

A proposed amendment becomes part of the Constitution as soon as it is ratified by three-fourths of the States (38 of 50 States). When the OFR verifies that it has received the required number of authenticated ratification documents, it drafts a formal proclamation for the Archivist to certify that the amendment is valid and has become part of the Constitution. This certification is published in the Federal Register and U.S. Statutes at Large and serves as official notice to the Congress and to the Nation that the amendment process has been completed.

This sounds like an extraordinary amount of work simply to insert the word "natural" immediately before each instance of the word "person." (It's only one word---but try diminishing the importance of that one word to a murder-case defendant when the jury returns a verdict of "guilty" versus "not guilty!")

But, again, remember that by accomplishing this seemingly-small process, a massive shift in America's laws and practices will occur. The idea of treating corporations the same as people will no longer have a legal foundation; the notion that corporations can spend all of their treasuries on political campaigns can be legislatively-barred; the concept that a multi-billion-dollar voice speaks with the same authority as that of a single person will be prohibited by law. In short, the false equivalency between humans and corporations will be banned from political life.

At the end of this process, the fundamental idea is about accountability. With the terrible decision (if it can be called that) in ***Santa Clara County v. Southern Pacific Railroad Co.***, the U.S. Supreme Court unleashed a torrent of laws and lawsuits that have fundamentally handicapped the political process in the United States for the last 132 years. That decision made corporations unaccountable in large part to the states and gave them political voice that they did not have for well over a century from the founding of this country.

By amending the 14th Amendment, we will take back the right to make corporations purely "creatures of statute," subject to the control of, and accountable to, the states. And by so doing, we will, once again, take charge of our own political destiny.

CHAPTER 6
ELIMINATE THE ELECTORAL COLLEGE

George W. Bush. Donald J. Trump. 'Nuff said. (However, look at Federalist No. 68, written by Alexander Hamilton, who proposed the creation of the Electoral College as a buffer between hot-headed, intemperate mobs and the election of the President. The difference between 1788 and now is that we have much better information available to us, via the Internet, and can---with a robust free press---make better electoral decisions.)

Realistically, we should be able to have a national vote for the Presidency. We have the technology and we certainly would be better served by having this style of voting. In that way, there would be a guarantee of "one person, one vote." And that would push out the voter suppression forces who try to engage in massive disenfranchisement on the basis of race, gender, or political party.

Circumstances have changed dramatically in the 200+ years since the Electoral College was created. Now, there are several good reasons for eliminating it.

- The Electoral College is fundamentally opposed to direct democracy. This is because it is based on a "winner-take-all" model. In all the states except Maine and Nebraska, the system means that a candidate with even 1 more popular vote gets all the EC votes. Hardly fair, right?
- The EC establishes a disparate representation. In small states, the EC gives voters far more representation. For example, in a small state such as Wyoming, the state has one electoral vote

for each 195,000 voters. By contrast, California has one electoral vote for each 712,000 voters.

- The Electors (the people who actually vote for the candidates) are loyal to what their parties say 99% of the time, and are not influenced by their consciences or what the will of the majority says. Again, this is antithetical to democratic principles.
- With the EC, candidates tend to campaign only in the large states and in the cities of those states, ignoring the small-population areas. Without the EC, candidates would need and want to campaign everywhere to get as many votes as possible.
- Of greatest importance, getting rid of the EC would make voters feel as though their votes count. This would increase the turnout because voters would feel like they had a real hand in electing a President. It would put teeth into the phrase, "one person, one vote."

CHAPTER 7
ELIMINATE JUDICIAL AND PROSECUTORIAL IMMUNITY

Judges and prosecutors should be able to be sued, albeit under restrictive circumstances. Post a bond, and the judge or prosecutor should be able to be sued.

Judicial immunity, and the related concept of prosecutorial immunity, stemmed from the notion of "the Divine Right of Kings," a quaint medieval concept that has no place in a modern society with concepts of accountability. The idea that the King could do no wrong had been adopted to protect judges and prosecutors from frivolous civil suits filed by losing defendants who wanted to make life miserable for the people who judged or prosecuted them. However, this rule has been used countless times to thwart genuinely-aggrieved defendants from seeking recourse against judges or prosecutors who engaged in misconduct.

For example, prosecutors are required under the rule in ***Brady v. Maryland***[8] to provide defense counsel with potentially exculpatory evidence. Those who fail to do so, intentionally, are deemed guilty of misconduct which could place an innocent defendant in jail and/or subject him/her to a fine, not to mention the possibility of the imposition of the death penalty in capital cases. Yet, if an innocent defendant has been wrongfully prosecuted, (s)he is seldom allowed to sue for monetary damages.

---

[8] *Brady v. Maryland* (1963) 373 U.S. 83

Higher courts have repeatedly prevented civil suits against prosecutors who decline to pursue justice in order to enhance their criminal prosecution record. This abhorrent practice happens more than thought, and precipitated the founding of The Innocence Project in 1992, which seeks to use DNA evidence to counter prosecutorial and/or judicial misconduct.

Even worse, a judge can engage in the most outrageous behavior and yet be completely immune from civil lawsuits. There have been cases in Michigan, Tennessee, New York, and California, to name but a few states, where judges have used their power to extort female parties---especially in family-law cases---into having sex with them. And there have been many other instances of judicial malfeasance going completely unpunished.

To those in favor of abolishing immunity, "Loosening the immunity doctrine would trigger a tsunami of lawsuits against judges, discourage appeals and strip judges of their independent decision-making authority---all of which would hurt the justice system," said Sheldon Nahmod, a constitutional law and civil rights professor at Chicago-Kent College of Law. (USA Today, July 28, 2014). They claim that judges and prosecutors would spend all their time looking over their shoulder and be afraid to use their "independent decision-making authority" in carrying out their duties.

Nonsense. And shame on a civil rights law professor for saying such foolish things.

It goes without saying that there would have to be some restrictions on the types of suits that could be brought; and it would be necessary for there to be panels of judges and prosecutors who would look at the initial statements of facts before allowing the suits to go forward. This gating procedure would naturally reduce the number of suits being litigated, but it would still send a loud and clear message: "No one is above the law."

And if innocent defendants were allowed to seek financial compensation, based on legitimate claims, then the bonding companies would handle the defenses of the judges and prosecutors. This system would certainly encourage these people to perform their jobs fairly, with competence, and with an eye towards doing what is right. The idea of judicial and prosecutorial accountability, if properly implemented, would reduce injustice and bring about a more effective legal system.

Injustice anywhere is a threat to justice everywhere. - Martin Luther King, Jr.

CHAPTER 8
QUADRUPLE THE SIZE
OF THE JUDICIARY

We need far more judges, judicial personnel, and courtrooms. In Los Angeles, one of the busiest court systems in the United States, we have seen many changes over the last 35-40 years. We used to have civil courts of limited jurisdiction (Municipal Courts) and those of unlimited jurisdiction (Superior Courts). The difference was based on the amount of money in controversy, i.e., how much was a person seeking in damages.

It used to cost just a few dollars to file a lawsuit, and if you were a defendant there was no charge to file your answer. Nowadays, the filing fees are hundreds of dollars---for both parties. All the fees have dramatically increased, and the number of judges has gone down.

There have been other radical alterations: special courts based on the type of case; major emphasis on mediation and arbitration instead of litigation; special training required of lawyers and judges for handling complex lawsuits; increased time before cases get to trial; massive changes in how Discovery disputes are resolved. The list goes on and on.

The judiciary is supposed to be the third, co-equal branch of government, yet it has clearly been given short-shrift. It costs far more to litigate these days, and you get far less "bang for your buck," legally speaking. Lawyers' fees and the surrounding costs have skyrocketed, but it takes much longer to get what purports to be "justice."

Justice delayed is justice denied. – William Gladstone, Prime Minister of England

---

We need to prioritize the delivery of legal services so that people can once again have faith that this is a nation of laws, "not of men." Without increasing the size of our judiciary---not just judges, but their clerks and other support staff; courtrooms and other support facilities; and all other aspects of the legal system---we will continue to punish people who are seeking civil or criminal justice.

Our judicial system might have served a country with a population of about 85 - 100 million people. However, our national population is about four times that amount. Shouldn't our judiciary expand to keep up with the demand for legal services? However, we also need to make major changes in how we deliver legal services. Transitioning from the adversarial (common law) to a civil-law type of judicial system may dramatically improve the way we administer law. That structural shift will be discussed in detail in the following chapter.

CHAPTER 9
CONVERT FROM A COMMON LAW TO A CIVIL-LAW JUDICIAL SYSTEM

The conversion from a common law to a civil-law judicial system would dramatically accelerate the processing of cases, and would get us away from the derivatives of 9th - 11th century Anglo-Saxon law, which is the basis of our legal system today.

(This system was extensively discussed in what has been called "the best book on English legal history," *The History of English Law Before the Time of Edward I*, Frederic William Maitland and Sir Frederick Pollock, 1895, <u>Cambridge University Press</u>. Portions of the following discussion come from that work.)

Anglo-American jurisprudence evolved from the systems prevailing in Western Germany and in England in the period from about 800 A.D. to the time of the Norman Conquest in 1066 A.D. Primitive forms of criminal justice applied, with the "wergild" (price paid for taking a man's life) being one of them, to differing types of trial.

Early versions of the adversary mode of seeking justice, based on one side versus the other, gradually gave way to a more sophisticated system. Trial by oath; trial by witness; or trial by ordeal; being forced to enter a plea in a court one thought had no power to hear the case against one, by an order of *peine forte et dure* ("punishment hard and long," with heavy stones/weights placed on you until you pled or you died); systems of gathering and using evidence; all evolved over the centuries to what we have today.

In modern American jurisprudence, law students are taught to review appellate cases on the basis of the FIRAC method. This acronym stands for Facts; Issue(s) of law; Rule(s) of Law; Analysis or Application of the Rules of Law to the facts; and the Conclusion. Our system, based on the English common law, is adversarial in nature. Each side had its position, and its advocate. Precedents, or the decision from previous cases, eventually were written down and relied upon by lawyers and by judges to provide a basis for the law that was common to all. Precedent (*stare decisis*, or "let the law stand on decided cases") was based on the notion that justice required that decisions in a newer case based on the same, or substantially similar, facts from previous cases should be decided the same way. The FIRAC method helped law students (and lawyers) understand precedent and how it should be used today.

Because the common law is adversarial, private counsel are used to advance and defend against causes of action in civil lawsuits. The justification for common law is the assumption that the adversarial method of litigation is most likely to produce a just result. The parties representing their sides will fight vigorously for their case position, and "justice will out."

Conversely, there is strong argument to suggest that because of the nature of the adversarial setting, litigants (through their lawyers) are taught to suppress evidence; obfuscate the issues; engage in psychological one-upsmanship; learn how to "game" the system; and corrupt the entire process of seeking justice.

By contrast, much of European (and some Asian) legal systems are "civil," that is, instead of a judge "finding the law" from cases or judicial precedent, civil-law judges rely on statutes as the basis for their findings and verdicts. Many transatlantic commentators have had chances to observe, compare, and contrast the two different legal systems. A good comparison and analysis of the two is derived from the writings of Charles H. Koch, Jr., Professor of Law at the William and Mary College of Law.[9] It is with much appreciation for his scholarly work that I have synthesized key arguments in his article.

1. At common law, advocacy and private representation are the guideposts of litigation. It is virtually impossible to impose meaningful public reform of the U.S. legal system since so much of it is based on privacy. The rules of the game simply do not allow it. In a civil law setting, the judiciary is a discrete and identifiable component of any legal system, and judicial conduct and performance can be subject to public scrutiny.

2. In civil law, judges are specially trained on how to be judges. They go through judging as a career path. They go to schools for judging; then go through apprenticeships, and gradually are promoted as the result of examinations, experience, and the views of the most seasoned judges. In short, being a judge is a career. By contrast, in England and the U.S., judges tend to be amateurs who first practiced law before transiting to the Bench. As a result, they bring many of their biases from their practice days to the Bench, which may not necessarily afford litigants the justice they seek.

3. Unlike the common law arena, civil law judges find the law from the codes enacted by the legislature. The legislature is seen as the most democratic aspect of society, so judges in a civil law setting are not allowed to judicially create law. A major criticism in the common law setting is the power that judges have to create law through bad decisions. A party who disagrees with the judge's decision has to go through great expense of time and money in pursuing an appeal; most appeals are denied, so the unhappy litigant is functionally remediless most of the time.

4. The common law requires the parties to develop the facts. As stated above, this results in the suppression of evidence, and gamesmanship as part of the advocacy process in many instances. Conversely, under the civil law, the judiciary investigates the facts.

---

[9] Prof. Charles H. Koch, Jr., *The Advantages of the Civil Law Judicial Design as the Model for Emerging Legal Systems*, Vol. 11, Iss. 1 of the <u>Indiana Journal of Global Legal Studies</u>, 2004.

Once the pleadings have been filed, the judges take over the case. They assign a special judicial officer to the case, and (s)he serves as the judge-*rapporteur*, responsible for building the record.

5. Unlike the common law, civil law litigation spreads most of the costs to society, thus getting rid of the huge money-based inequality seen in the U.S. At civil law, "parties are ultimately billed for the costs of the expert. Still, there is a savings in that they need only pay for experts sufficient to satisfy the judge rather than redundant experts to counteract their opponents' experts. Moreover, a reforming system might consider public financing." (Koch, fn. 68)

6. The common law constantly insists on the jury as a fundamental form of protection, yet only about 5% of criminal cases and about 1% of civil cases are heard by juries in the U.S.[10] In the civil law countries, fact finding is conducted by judges. So is the rendering of a judicial decision.

We have many specialized proceedings here in the United States, especially the administrative hearings. These courts can and do render legal decisions regularly, without juries, and with one or multiple judges being the decision makers.

Changing the legal structure from common law to civil law would certainly not take place overnight, but we have enough progressives in and out of the legal system in the U.S. to help promote this agenda. It would bring back a sense of justice (or perhaps instill it where there was none before); it would reduce costs; it would save time; it would provide a much fairer way of trying both criminal and civil matters; and it would produce a sense that we are working to bring more benefits to our citizens than to the plutocrats.

---

[10] Abrahamson, Jeffrey, "We, the Jury: The Jury System and the Ideal of Democracy," p. 252 (2000).

CHAPTER 10
MORE STATES, MORE/BETTER SUPREME COURT JUSTICES

Some writers have asked the fundamental question: why can't we have more states?

For example, Puerto Rico is American, but it lacks the basic franchise rights that states have. It needs to be a state.

Likewise, why can't Washington, D.C. enjoy the status of statehood? Its present condition is ridiculous, politically speaking. It needs to be a state.

Then, the elephant in the room is the question of what to do about California.

California has the fifth largest economy in the world, now larger than that of the United Kingdom[11]. California is considering succession from the United States ("Calexit," sponsored by Louis J. Marinelli of "YesCalifornia.org), and is looking for a vote on succession during a special election in 2021. The odds of the "YesCalifornia" movement appear to be somewhat dim, according to recent polls showing a more than 2-1 opposition to succession.[12]

---

[11] *California Now has the World's 5th Largest Economy*, Associated Press, May 4, 2018

[12] Berkeley Institute of Government Studies Poll, March 2017.

Among the many reasons given by the pro-secessionists is the notion that our taxes paid to Washington, D.C. far exceed the benefits gotten back. In short, Californians pay more than they get; have to deal with policies with which they do not agree; and have significant cultural differences with the rest of the United States.[13]

In the alternative to "CalExit," a Silicon Valley billionaire, Tim Draper, has sponsored "Cal 3," a political movement to split California into three states: Northern California; Southern California; and California. That one was approved to be on the November 6, 2018 general election ballot, but the State Supreme Court denied it and forced it off the ballot.

Had Cal 3's campaign succeeded, we would have an additional four U.S. Senators. Add two for Puerto Rico and two more for Washington, D.C., and that constitutes an eight percent increase in the Senate's population.

These eight potential Senators (and their corresponding Representatives) would likely be more progressive than the bulk of the existing members of Congress, thus shifting the political strengths and alliances in that body for an extended period.

However, it is not merely Congressional change that is important, but the composition of the U.S. Supreme Court which is essential.

We have seen with the recent confirmation of Brett Kavanaugh to the U.S. Supreme Court that Trump has absolutely no compunction about promoting right-wingers who can contaminate the judiciary for generations.

Because the size of the Supreme Court is not fixed by the Constitution but is set by Congress, we have an opportunity to elect progressives who would be willing to add to the Supreme Court's bench.

President Franklin D. Roosevelt proposed adding six justices to the Supreme Court, and was subject to the criticism that he was attempting to neutralize the anti-progressive judges who fought the

---

[13] *People in California are Calling for a 'Calexit" From the US in the Face of a Trump Win*, Melia Robinson, <u>Business Insider</u>, November 9, 2016.

legislation he and his Congressional allies devised to address the serious problems arising from the Depression. Two months after his proposal, two Supreme Court justices joined the liberals and upheld the laws establishing the National Labor Relations Board and the Social Security Act. The need for the so-called "court packing plan" was deemed moot, and it was voted down by Congress in July 1937.

Nonetheless, it is well within the ambit of Congressional authority to add to the judicial bench and give Democrats a better chance of obtaining judicial approval for progressive legislation that would benefit the Middle Class and the poor rather than the top 1/100ths of the top 1%, as is the Court's present mandate.

While we are on the subject of Supreme Court justices, is there a legitimate reason these days for keeping the justices on the court for life? Is there a Constitutional mandate that requires that Supreme Court justices' terms be for life?

The Founding Fathers wanted to insulate the Supreme Court justices from political passions. The Founders feared that in practical terms we newly-coined Americans would turn into an ochlocracy. Their solution was to provide the justices with life-long tenure. But that was at a time when the average life-span for men was in the low-to-mid-'40s, so a judge appointed to the high court at the age of 35 would likely die before the age of 45, too young to do much damage for many years.

However, with today's medical technology, prescription drugs, and improved lifestyles, it is entirely possible that a person born in the 1960s could easily live until the age of 90. Judicial appointees could have a tenure on the bench of 30, 40, or even 50 years. What would be wrong with that? Here are some concerns.

- **Decrepitude** (mental and/or physical incapacity, and unwillingness to retire)
- **Intellectual autopilot** (as people get older, they tend to become more mentally fixed, detracting from the open-minded quality necessary for good judging)
- **Hubristic complacency** ("Power corrupts, and absolute power corrupts absolutely." Justices can become arrogant with more time on the bench)

- **Unaccountability** (with fewer appointments possible because of increased lifespans, longer tenure reduces the chance for presidents and senators to provide the only form of democratic accountability consistent with judicial independence)
- **Randomness** (the longevity of individual justices may thwart the ability of presidents to appoint jurists who might hang on to challenge presidents they don't like)
- **Uglier confirmation battles** (with longer tenure, conservatives hope, and liberals fear, that President Trump may lock in a young, conservative majority that could revolutionize constitutional law for 20 to 40 years. And the Senate has been particularly antagonistic to former President Obama, refusing to even give a hearing to Judge Merrick Garland, though highly qualified)
- **Eroded legitimacy** (lifelong tenure means that justices are unlikely to revisit controversial decisions. With stubborn adherence to bad law, the high court may make people have less trust and confidence in the Court, and trust the judicial process less and less)
- **Diminished productivity** (Supreme Court justices have reduced their number of opinions, and are likely to continue to do so. This would reduce the likelihood of hearing important, but not necessarily "exciting," cases)[14]

Legal scholars have proposed changing the appointment process so that judicial nominees would be subject to terms of 18 years. This suggestion would solve the problems described above[15]

Again, the problem of lifetime appointments could be changed in the Senate, and would likely receive support from the progressives who entered Congress in November 2018.

---

[14] *Life Tenure is Too Long for Supreme Court Justices*, Stuart Taylor, Jr., <u>The Atlantic</u>, June 2005

[15] *Term Limits for the Supreme Court: Life Tenure Reconsidered*, Profs. Steven G. Calabresi and James Lindgren, <u>Harvard Journal of Law and Public Policy</u>, Vol. 29, No. 3, 2006

CHAPTER 11
ABOLISH PRIVATE GUN OWNERSHIP (REPEAL THE 2ND AMENDMENT)

The 2nd Amendment, for much of the time of our country's existence, was not held to establish personal gun ownership as a sacrosanct Constitutional right. Its current political orientation is derived only from a decade-old Supreme Court case, and yet those who advocate gun ownership do so with the zealotry of the European knights seeking to retake Jerusalem during the Crusades.

We have a massive obsession with guns in this country. It is costing us hundreds of billions of dollars a year in lives, destroyed families, law enforcement costs, and reduced workplace productivity. In short, it's a cancer that is eating away at our society. What is the solution?

<u>REPEAL THE 2ND AMENDMENT.</u>

Yes, I said it. If we don't stop our gun fetish, we're going to continue to turn into what President Trump has called "a s***hole country."

We have had an increasing number of mass shootings over the last 20 or so years. Not surprisingly, mothers are especially hard-hit when they lose a child to a senseless gunshot death.

Nicole Hockley is only one of the dozens of Connecticut parents whose life was shredded when Adam Lanza walked into the Sandy Hook elementary school and began killing students and faculty. "For the first year after losing Dylan, I felt shame and guilt if I even smiled. But you have to find a way to let those feelings come back. I hope to someday. I'm not there yet."

Twenty-six people died at Sandy Hook, including 20 elementary-aged students. President Obama has called the mass shooting the worst day of his presidency. "I thought I knew what pain looked like," Hockley said as she described telling Dylan's brother what happened. "The first image that comes to my mind when I think about pain now is Jake's face when my husband told him that Dylan had been killed. He just howled. I'd never heard a child make that kind of noise before."

On a personal note, I have been robbed at gunpoint twice in my life; those were not fun experiences. As a near-teen, I almost was killed by a former mental patient who had a military rifle.

When I was 12 years old, visiting my relatives in Indianapolis during the summer, my now-deceased older cousin, Fred, and I walked down the alley behind his home. A couple of blocks away, there was a back yard with a chain-link fence, and behind that fence was a big, bad Chow. Fred thought it would be "fun" if I were to throw a cherry-bomb into the back yard and scare the dog. He gave me a cherry bomb and some matches; voila! Mission accomplished. The dog went nuts. Fred had to run back home to get some more fireworks.

While I stayed in front of the fence, watching the dog continue to angrily bark at me, I didn't hear the dog's owner creep up behind me. You can imagine I was pretty shocked when the owner put the muzzle of an assault rifle behind my right ear. In a tearful voice, the owner told me to say my prayers because he was going to blow my head off.

Fortunately, Fred arrived in time and was able to calm the neighbor down. Had he not timely arrived, my mother, hell, my entire family would have had a major tragedy on their hands. Was I stupid for exploding a cherry bomb in the guy's back yard? Obviously, I was. But---and this is the critical part---the man had been in a mental institution for over a decade, according to Fred, and yet he had no problem acquiring an assault rifle.

In spite of knowledge of Sandy Hook, Columbine, Margery Stoneman Douglas, and countless other tragedies, sportsmen's lodges, gun clubs, and hunting associations funnel their members' private monies into the campaigns of pro-guns political candidates.

There is perhaps no stronger argument for removing private funds to support public functions, such as elections, than the existence of the National Rifle Association ("NRA"). This group, full of people who believe in the sovereignty of guns, rifles, and all things that go "bang," loudly proclaims as inviolate Americans' "rights to own guns." They pour many millions of dollars into the campaign coffers of politicians throughout the land, from the Presidential campaign all the way down to local races for schoolboard members. And to what end?

This country has had a psychotic fixation on guns for many years. The NASCAR-watching, beer-guzzling, gun-toters have a pernicious love for things that kill or seriously injure people. They say, "Well, it's in the Constitution." Not so fast. It was not that many years ago (on June 26, 2008) that the U.S. Supreme Court ruled in ***District of Columbia vs. Heller***[16], squeaking by in a narrow 5-4 decision, that the right of gun ownership was individual, and not connected to service in a militia or military force.

Prior to that, for the nearly 220 years since the passage of the 2nd Amendment to the U.S. Constitution did the Supreme Court view gun ownership as a kind of "collective right," to help counterbalance the coercive and possibly dictatorial forces of a too-powerful central government.

Nowadays, the gun nuts—let's call them by their proper names— caress their precious pistols, and stroke their redemptive rifles in an almost sexual way. If you propose strict gun controls, it's as if you were threatening them with castration. They claim that gun ownership is a "God-given right."

Bushwa.

---

[16] *District of Columbia v. Heller* (2008) 554 U.S. 570

The 2nd Amendment was written by a man, and it can be changed accordingly. Seriously: does anyone *really* need guns, rifles, AR-15s, M-1s, or any of the other forms of firearms that flood the markets and turn our streets into *abattoirs*?

The 2nd Amendment Was Based on Maintaining Slavery

In the South, long before the Revolutionary War, slave-patrol militias in Georgia, the Carolinas, and Virginia were mandated by law: men between 18 and 45 had to be members of "slave militias," and were required to monitor slaves' quarters and activities on a regular basis. It was deemed essential for safety, because there had been a number of slave rebellions, and the slave-owners wanted to maintain the institution of slavery by whip and at the point of a gun[17].

The author of what became the 2nd Amendment was James Madison, the "Father of the Constitution." He had been urged by Thomas Jefferson to prepare amendments to the Constitution. His colleagues among the Founding Fathers---Patrick Henry, George Mason, and James Monroe---were all slaveholders and were afraid that the first version of the 2nd Amendment to the Constitution would give the federal government too much power to abolish slaves. At their strong insistence, it was deemed necessary to achieve a compromise between the federal and the states' power.

The original draft of the 2nd Amendment read: "The right of the people to keep and bear arms shall not be infringed; a well armed, and well regulated militia being the best security of a free country: but no person religiously scrupulous of bearing arms, shall be compelled to render military service in person."

At the ratifying convention in Virginia in 1788, Patrick Henry expressed great fear of the imbalance in power between the federal and the state governments. He was especially worried that the proposed ability of the federal government to create and regulate

---

[17] *Slave Patrols: Law and Violence in Virginia and the Carolinas,* Sally E. Hadden (2001, Harvard Historical Studies).

militias would overwhelm the states, including their abilities to maintain and regulate slave militias.

The slave-owners were afraid that the grant of such power to the federal government would dramatically reduce (or eliminate) the power of slave-patrols/slave militias, so they demanded a significant change, resulting in this version of the 2nd Amendment: "A well regulated Militia, being necessary to the security of a free State, the right of the people to keep and bear Arms, shall not be infringed."

This is the version now in the Bill of Rights.

Sadly, the gun-owning mindset has been so deeply ingrained in our social psyche that it is part of our DNA. The sense that we "need" guns---lots of them, and easily obtained---is pervasive throughout many parts of our society.

We need to start a serious, prolonged, and **deep** conversation about our so-called "need" for guns. Other societies, such as Australia, Japan, England, Germany, to name but a few of the many who have chosen to stop the madness, don't find that gun ownership or possession equals masculinity. Women don't have to prove how tough they are by getting a Glock or securing a Smith & Wesson.

And since so much talk in this country is based on dollars and cents, let's have that discussion. According to a recent article in the Washington Post[18], the cost of gun violence in this country *every year* is about $229 **BILLION**. That figure comes from a major study prepared by the Giffords Law Center to Prevent Gun Violence. (lawcenter.giffords.org) which has accumulated massive statistics on how much gun violence costs us in this country.

That comes out to about $700 per year for every man, woman and child in the United States. That's a cost of about $60/month for every man, woman and child.

And, in the aftermath of the mass shooting in Las Vegas on October 1, 2017, CBS *Moneywatch*'s Aimee Picchi wrote that, "gun violence in the U.S. also has an enormous financial cost, rippling through the economy in the form of lost wages, medical bills, higher taxes for law

---

[18] "The Enormous Economic Cost of Gun Violence" (Washington Post, Michelle Singletary, February 28, 2018)

enforcement and lower property values, among other factors." She went on to say: "The economic devastation caused by gun violence tends to get overlooked because Americans may not think it impacts them, especially if they live in a safe neighborhood or away from cities beset with crime,....Yet taxpayers are picking up the bill by paying for the medical care of victims on Medicaid and by forking out more in taxes to fund law enforcement, the criminal justice system, and jails and prisons."

In short, we've **got to get over** this absolutely ***absurd*** notion that guns equal protection, safety, and/or fun. They are instruments of death, plain and simple. If people are that enthused about Death or injury, let them be free to jump off of bridges or tall buildings or indulge in any number of forms of suicide. Just don't allow them the opportunity to take me, or other innocent people, with them.

And above all else, we have to prevent the purveyors of Death and Destruction, that is, the NRA, from making political campaign contributions and continuing the pattern of brainwashing Americans into thinking that gun ownership and possession is as American as apple pie. Stop the madness, and start supporting life.

They've abolished private gun ownership in Australia, and there's no reason why we couldn't and shouldn't do it here in America. Think of the family and friendship tragedies that would be averted, and the monumental treasure to be saved.

On Friday, August 3, 2018, in court documents, the NRA pled that it was facing terrible financial burdens based on fines and penalties it was paying in New York State; it uttered dire warnings that it could not long survive in its present form.

Needless to say, Twitter went crazy, with countless numbers of people Tweeting their "thoughts and prayers" to the organization.

CHAPTER 12
A HUMANE, COMMON-SENSE APPROACH TO THE DEATH PENALTY

The 8th Amendment has been invoked countless times to challenge the constitutionality of imposing the death penalty in capital cases. It can be argued that there is a "death penalty industry" within the legal profession, consisting of proponents and opponents, both arguing the merits of their positions. The prosecution, imprisonment, appeals, and imposition of the death sentence takes years, often decades, and ties up the courts in many arguments, especially the ones related to the 8th Amendment's prohibition against "cruel and unusual punishment" due to pain or other types of "cruel and unusual" suffering prior to and/or during the execution of the condemned prisoner. Literally hundreds of millions of dollars are spent by the states over the years in addressing these issues. One state has come up with a solution that merits serious consideration.

In my book, Oklahoma hasn't had a lot to brag about: not economically, socially, politically, or culturally. However, it is doing something that I have advocated for the better part of the last quarter-century. Going forward, it has pledged to use nitrogen hypoxia (asphyxiation) as the method of executing convicted defendants in death-penalty cases.

Some will recall that lethal injection has been problematic in Texas and in Oklahoma for years. **Hospira**----the sole United States manufacturer of sodium thiopental----has stopped producing it, and there is a world-wide shortage based on an increasing number of countries' restrictions on the use of drugs in executions. Several states have switched from the three-drug "cocktail" for lethal injections to a single dose of pentobarbital, a drug used to euthanize animals.

However, that is a new procedure and may face a number of legal challenges at both the state and federal levels on the grounds that it may not pass the 8th Amendment's prohibition against "cruel or unusual" punishment. The main concern in previous pleadings opposing lethal injections, as well as the use of hanging; the electric chair; the firing squad; and the gas chamber, is that each method has the tendency to cause unnecessary pain and/or physical torture.

In other words, much of the objection to the imposition of capital punishment has been based on the U.S. Constitution's 8th Amendment, which prohibited "cruel and unusual punishments."

In examining the 8th Amendment basis for challenging the death penalty, the U.S. Supreme Court found in *Furman v. Georgia*[19] that capital punishment throughout the United States was "cruel and unusual punishment," in violation of the U.S. Constitution's 8th Amendment. The high Court struck capital punishment throughout the country for four years because of 8th Amendment objections.

In 1976, in *Gregg v. Georgia*[20] the U.S. Supreme Court held that Georgia's new capital punishment procedures (bifurcated trials and automatic appeals) were in accordance with the 8th Amendment. Thus, *Furman's* universal prohibition against capital punishment was stricken, on the basis of some states' assurances of "greater Due Process" in (A) imposing the death penalty, and (B) imposing capital punishment.

In the intervening years, a number of states have moved from the older, more violent modes of executing a condemned defendant (shooting, electric chair, hanging) to less violent means (gas chambers or lethal injection).

As indicated above, however, the lone U.S. manufacturer of sodium thiopental has stopped making it, and European manufacturers

---

[19] *Furman v. Georgia* (1972) 408 U.S. 238
[20] *Gregg v. Georgia* (1976) 428 U.S. 153

have been its export to the United States. Thus, lethal injections are functionally non-options in America.

Oklahoma has many options in terms of the administration of the capital punishment. However, it conducted a recent study[21] which showed that death by nitrogen-induced hypoxia would solve many problems in executing condemned murderers.

The results were adopted by Oklahoma in mid-March 2018 and the State is now working on the protocols for implementing this procedure.

What is particularly significant about nitrogen asphyxiation is that it boasts six advantages that other means of capital punishment lack. As stated in the Copeland-Parr-Papas study cited above (p. 2):

1. An execution protocol that induced hypoxia via nitrogen inhalation would be a humane method to carry out a death sentence.

2. Death sentence protocols carried out using nitrogen inhalation would not require assistance from any licensed medical professionals.

3. Death sentences carried out by nitrogen inhalation would be simple to administer.

4. Nitrogen is readily available for purchase and sourcing would not pose a difficulty.

5. Death sentences carried out by nitrogen inhalation would not depend upon the cooperation of the offender being executed.

6. Use of nitrogen as a method of execution can assure a quick and painless death of the offender.

---

[21] *Nitrogen Induced Hypoxia as a Form of Capital Punishment,* by Michael Copeland, J.D.; Tom Parr, M.S.; and Christine Papas, J.D., Ph.D.

A gas mask with a nearby nitrogen-containing bottle could easily be placed on the head of the offender, and it would not have to be administered by a doctor, many of whom will not participate because of the Hippocratic Oath they have taken: "Do No Harm."

A prison guard could easily administer the procedure.

It should also be noted that nitrogen is available everywhere. Cost is negligible and there would be no basis for companies to stop its sale.

Even if a convict did not want to cooperate, placing him in a chair with appropriate restraints would render his obstructive efforts futile.

In a few seconds, the convict would lose consciousness and would not suffer any of the agonies associated with conventional gas-chamber executions. Using nitrogen, the offender would be able to exhale carbon dioxide and would not feel any of the acidosis normally experienced by asphyxiation. Within 30 seconds, he would be well on his way to death, and within three-four minutes at most a doctor would be able to pronounce him dead.

In 1995, in <u>The National Review</u>, Stuart Creque authored an article dealing with the 8th Amendment's prohibition against "cruel and unusual punishment.[22] Creque's seminal article on this topic was in

---

[22] Stuart Creque, *Killing With Kindness: Capital Punishment by Nitrogen Asphyxiation* (<u>The National Review</u>, 1995)

response to a 9th Circuit U.S. District Court decision that California's gas chamber was an unconstitutionally cruel and unusual punishment. The article suggested nitrogen could provide a simple and painless alternative to the gas chamber that would require no elaborate medical procedures to administer.

In addition to the use of nitrogen asphyxiation as a form of capital punishment, it was also advocated by Derek Humphry[23], a leader in the assisted-suicide movement for the terminally-ill. Both Mr. Humphry and those in the "Final Exit Network" of people suffering from costly, painful, and inevitably-terminal illnesses have advocated the use of inert gases (nitrogen or helium) as a means of quickly and peacefully committing suicide to alleviate their suffering and the suffering of loved ones.

One of the greatest tragedies is to know that a loved one is suffering from an incurable illness or a condition in which death will be prefaced by long periods of pain and suffering, and that there is nothing that can be done about it. Mr. Humphrey, the late Dr. Jack Kevorkian aka "Dr. Death," and others felt that voluntary euthanasia applied to suffering and terminally ill people was the humane way to give them death with dignity.

To those who have suffered the moral torment of wanting capital punishment, on the one hand, but who were loath to implement it in its conventional forms, on the other hand, this method—--progressive, apparently constitutional on both the state and federal levels (although some rabidly anti-death penalty lawyers and groups would no doubt file suits challenging that proposition), inexpensive, and easy to administer without all the pain and torment typically seen in lethal injections and gas chamber executions—--would provide a possible basis to resume executions without the hand-wringing associated with 8th Amendment concerns.

A survey of state and federal court opinions in capital cases reveals that many decisions were procedurally-based: there were problems

---

[23] **Derek Humphry,** *Final Exit: the Practicalities of Self-Deliverance and Assisted Suicide for the Dying* (<u>Random House LLC</u> 2002)

with the police investigation; the way the prosecution conducted the trial; the failure to provide the defendant with adequate defenses or make available greater resources for his defense; and other matters that revolved around the fairness (or unfairness) of the prosecution as a whole.

Other cases, however, have examined the actual protocols and procedures used in administering capital punishment. Some have looked at the question of whether a defendant knew or understood that the prosecution against him would potentially lead to the death penalty, while a number of cases have examined the mechanics of executing a prisoner.

The bulk of cases dealing with the means of killing a defendant have addressed the fundamental concerns of the 8th Amendment: was the means of execution such that it was "cruel" or "unusual?" Was the method going to (or was it likely to) create such pain, suffering, or torment that in the eyes of most people it would be repugnant to the consciences of civilized beings to impose this penalty on the condemned (wo)man?

With no pain, no cruelty, simply allowing the convict to "go to sleep, and not wake up," the administration of the death penalty through nitrogen asphyxiation would bypass the 8th Amendment concerns and give death penalty advocates a stronger justification for returning to the imposition of the death penalty.

Moreover, the cost of capital punishment versus life imprisonment is a serious part of the conversation. A major study was recently performed, and it was shown that, across the U.S., the cost of capital punishment was a little over a million dollars more than imprisoning the defendant for life without the possibility of parole. The additional costs were predicated on the number of appeals available to state and federal prisoners, to ensure that the defendant had been afforded the additional Due Process benefits articulated in the *Furman* decision[24].

---

[24] McFarland, Torin, *The Death Penalty vs. Life Incarceration: A Financial Analysis* (<u>Susquehanna University Political Review</u>: Vol. 7, Article 4, 2016)

Considering that nitrogen asphyxiation would be quick, painless, and free of the possible administrative errors to which the other means of capital punishment were subject, it might be time to revisit the topic of the death penalty, and the question of the number of appeals and the reasons for the delays in executing a capital case defendant. At least from both an economic and an 8th Amendment perspective, nitrogen asphyxiation would seem to make more sense than our present methods of imposing capital punishment.

Those in favor of imposing the death penalty claim that it is a deterrent; that it brings closure to the victim's family and/or friends; and that it represents society's implementation of justice. Those against it note that it does not deter, since most violent crimes, especially murder, are committed on the basis of emotional impulse and not rational pre-planning; mental health professionals often note that executions do not bring about closure, whereas psychotherapy much more frequently helps; and imposition of the death penalty is hypocritical, since on the one hand we say that murder is a grave crime, yet we commit a form of murder when we execute the condemned person.

Naturally, a strong discussion would still be necessary to determine whether it would ever be morally justifiable to impose the death penalty, but at least the 8th Amendment grounds for challenging it would no longer exist, and the reduction of costs would certainly be available if all the years' worth of defendants waiting on Death Row could be eliminated through the reduction of superfluous appellate procedures.

SUMMARY OF PART I DO-ABLES

Some readers may be novices to civic engagement; others may have intermediate, or even advanced, experience. For the latter, please forgive the basic instructions here.

When I refer to "letter-writing," I include both printed correspondence as well as e-mails.

MeetUp is a nine-year-old on-line community. Go to your computer, type in "MeetUp.com," and you'll be invited to open a free account. You'll be able to search for communities for all kinds of interests: yodeling; model railroads; hiking; protecting a nearby park; and so much more. One important caveat: please don't be one of those socially-averse people who joins MeetUp right after the New Year, only to never attend a meeting. If you have problems getting out, make that one of your New Year's Resolutions: you'll actually <u>do</u> what you promise yourself you'll do. It's a great feeling of accomplishment when that happens.

For neighborhood groups, you may see notes on the local grocery store bulletin board, or you might hear something from one of your neighbors. If you live in an apartment, your lobby may have a bulletin board which lists activities you might be interested in. Heck, you might want to start a conversation with a neighbor; find out about him or her; and see if there are common interests between you.

You can use Google to check into ACLU.org; National Lawyers Guild; Common Cause; feminist organizations; environmental groups; and so on. Talk to people at work and find out what they're doing or interested in. You might find out what you like; join and give it a shot.

Go to https://www.usa.gov/elected-officials/ to get a complete list of contact information for all your elected officials.

Below are areas of possible interests, and some positive steps you can take to add your talents to what they're doing.

REMOVE PRIVATE MONEY FROM POLITICS

- ☑ Through MeetUp, party- and neighborhood groups, ACLU, National Lawyers Guild, and many other reformist organizations, add your voice to the mix. Letter-writing, phone calls, and visits to state and Congressional offices. Make sure that you add your friends and family to the effort, too. With enough persistence, change will come.
- ☑

TACKLE PRESSING PROBLEMS OF THE ENVIRONMENT, INEQUALITY, ENTITLEMENTS, AND FAMILY VALUES

- ☑ Gather up friends, family, people from MeetUps, and responsible organizations. Engage in letter-writing, phone calls, and visits to your local, state and federal offices. Let your elected officials know that they must perform---or they're out of office (see Chapter 4).
- ☑ Form "Asteroid Clubs," locally, to start educational programs in and out of the schools.

ADD "NATURAL" BEFORE "PERSON" IN THE 14TH AMENDMENT

- ☑ This calls for a Constitutional Convention or followup on the state legislative level (see Chapter 5). Gather up friends, family, and people from MeetUps, party- and neighborhood groups. Engage in letter-writing, phone calls, and visits to state and Congressional offices. Don't let your legislators rest until they know you mean business.

ELIMINATE THE ELECTORAL COLLEGE

☑ This also calls for a Constitutional Convention or followup on the state legislative level (see Chapter 6). Gather up friends, family, and people from MeetUps, party- and neighborhood groups. Engage in letter-writing, phone calls, and visits to state and Congressional offices. Don't let your legislators rest until they take care of business---*your* business.

ELIMINATE JUDICIAL AND PROSECUTORIAL IMMUNITY

☑ Gather up friends, family, and people from MeetUps, party- and neighborhood groups. Engage in letter-writing, phone calls, and visits to your local (city council) and state (assembly and senate) offices. Let your elected officials know that they must perform---or they're out of office (see Chapter 7).

QUADRUPLE THE SIZE OF THE JUDICIARY

☑ Through MeetUp, party- and neighborhood groups, ACLU, National Lawyers Guild, and many other reformist organizations and consumer-advocacy groups, initiate or participate in letter-writing, phone calls, and visits to your state (assembly and senate) offices. (See Chapter 8.)

CONVERT FROM A COMMON LAW TO A CIVIL LAW JUDICIAL SYSTEM

☑ Through MeetUp, party- and neighborhood groups, ACLU, National Lawyers Guild, and many other reformist organizations and consumer-advocacy groups, initiate or participate in letter-writing, phone calls, and visits to your state (assembly and senate) offices. (See Chapter 9.)

MORE STATES, MORE/BETTER SUPREME COURT JUSTICES

☑ Through MeetUp, party- and neighborhood groups, ACLU, National Lawyers Guild, and many other reformist organizations and consumer-advocacy groups, initiate or participate in letter-writing, phone calls, and visits to your federal (congressperson's and senator's) offices (see Chapter 10).

ABOLISH PRIVATE GUN OWNERSHIP (REPEAL THE 2ND AMENDMENT)

☑ Through student-, family-, physician-, and many other reformist organizations [see Internet for literally hundreds of listings], initiate or participate in letter-writing, phone calls, and visits to your federal (congressperson's and senator's) offices (see Chapter 11). Until the personal "right" to bear arms is removed, your legislators haven't done their jobs.

REFORM CAPITAL PUNISHMENT

☑ Through MeetUp, party- and neighborhood groups, ACLU, National Lawyers Guild, and many other reformist organizations and consumer-advocacy groups, initiate or participate in letter-writing, phone calls, and visits to your state (assembly and senate) and federal (congressperson's and senator's) offices. (See Chapter 12.)

PART II
THE BASES OF OUR ECONOMY AND TAXES

CHAPTER 13
THE SOCIO-POLITICAL BASES FOR AMERICA'S ECONOMY AND TAXES

The economy of the United States has dramatically shifted in the 240+ years since the signing of the Declaration of Independence. Prior to our divorce from England, we were simply a set of colonies that had started out as chartered settlements in the early 1600s. We were largely agricultural, with a few trading ports here and there along the eastern seaboard.

Over the decades, American farmers used British troops (and sometimes their own firepower) to displace the native Americans who had been on this continent for thousands of years. These naked land grabs, starting in the 1600s, eventually led to two greatly immoral consequences, spread out over hundreds of years: the genocidal treatment of the Indians, and the importation of hundreds of thousands of African slaves.

According to historian David Hackett Fischer, in his masterful 1989 novel *Albion's Seed*[25], there were four waves of migrants from England spread out from the early 1600s to the mid-1700s: the **Puritans** (mostly from East Anglia, northeast of London), who settled in Massachusetts; the **Cavaliers**, who were members of the nobility (mostly from the south of England), who settled in Virginia, along with many thousands of indentured servants; the **Quakers**, who settled in Pennsylvania; and the so-called "**Scots-Irish**," (who were neither Scottish nor Irish, but who lived on the border between England and Scotland), and who settled in the western parts of the

---

[25] David Hackett Fisher, *Albion's Seed: Four British Folkways* (Oxford University Press, 1989)

Carolinas, Virginia, Tennessee, and Georgia (collectively, "Appalachia").

Together, these groups were as religiously- and culturally-diverse as one could imagine. They took their prejudices and passions to the New World, and they were not at all a monolithic cultural entity, but lived almost as if they were from completely different societies. The Puritans were better-educated than anyone else in England; the Quakers were religiously and socially tolerant; the Cavaliers were landed nobility, which instituted the "plantation" system which spread throughout the South; and the Scots-Irish were the descendants of the poorly- or uneducated border clans who lived insular lives and felt little to no allegiance to any government.

Politically, it can be argued that the intellectual development of the Puritans, coupled with the tolerance of the Quakers, gave rise to the Eastern Liberals. On the other hand, the Cavaliers were the New World's aristocracy. Their allies, politically, were the freedom-at-any-cost Scots-Irish/Appalachians. The Cavaliers didn't want any government authorities interfering with their slave-holding plantation life, while the Appalachians were descended from peoples who, for hundreds of years in northern England, bore the brunt of brutal policies at the hands of English and Scottish monarchs, and who distrusted both sides of the Border. So the Cavaliers and the Appalachians formed their own conservative alliance, with a goal of having little or no government interference in their ways of life here in the New World.

There was much to learn about life in the New World. The English colony at Jamestown, Virginia was a military outpost, consisting almost exclusively of men. They suffered starvation, and of the 100 colonists, 40 starved to death. Powhatan, the Indian chief ruling the area around Jamestown, was not keen on "illegal aliens" coming in, stealing land, interfering with their way of life, and creating a foreign culture in the midst of the land of plenty.

Eventually, shiploads of English colonists came over in the 1620s and 1630s, laden with indentured servants from England. Labor was in extremely short supply in Virginia, and it was vitally important to have as many hands as possible to work on the farms throughout the Virginia Colony.

At about the same time as the development of tobacco crops that were particularly well-suited for Virginia, African slaves began to be imported into New Amsterdam (New York) and then into Virginia. By the 1640s and 1650s, the English slave trade was beginning to take off, stimulated by the phenomenal rise in tobacco planting. The labor shortage was not going to be ameliorated by using Native Americans, since, to the British colonists, the Indians could and would easily abscond with products and move back to and blend with the local tribes.

By the 1660s and 1670s, there was another Great Plague, and the need for local laborers in London for construction projects needed in the aftermath of the fires was so great that it was virtually impossible to get indentured servants. It was in that time period, too, that South Carolina became a Chartered Colony, with massive immigration from Barbados. South Carolina's founders came to "Charles Town" (Charleston) with an economic perspective completely based on slavery, and their efforts to ramp up their own production of tobacco and other agricultural products was directly tied into increased imports of African slaves.

During the period from the 1660s to the Civil War (1861-1865), the American South developed agriculture as its number one product and source of income. It had developed a system of laws designed to benefit the white settlers and land grabbers and dominate and decimate the Native Americans, on the one hand, and enslave Africans and their descendants, on the other.

The period from the 1760s to 1830, in Europe and America, was known as "the Industrial Revolution." Mechanical inventions relating to the processing of cotton (the cotton gin), transportation (the steam engine), weaving (mechanical looms), and many other forms of manufacturing, dramatically increased the ability to supply and distribute goods. The Industrial Revolution, in turn, spurred the creation of whole new industries, most of which were located in the Northeastern United States.

The economic disparities between the South and the North in the U.S. were small, at first. However, a number of trends developed at about the same time, and gave manufacturing the economic edge: more education, efficiencies of scale, the ability to develop factories and run them on multiple shifts, and political affiliations that favored the wealthier manufacturers, all led to increased regional tensions between the North and the South.

Much ado has been made about slavery's gross immorality, but there was also an economic component to the stress between North and South. Arguments have been made in recent years that American slavery depended in large part on capitalism. In his book[26], Calvin Schermerhorn made the point that the South needed slaves, but had little cash money to pay for them. The North had money, and needed ventures that would employ that money.

As is almost always the case, money can be a great motivator for innovations in human activity that can create more money. The North had money, but had to find places to deploy it for profit; the South needed slaves, but had little cash to pay for them. What was to be done to create a benefit for both sides?

---

[26] **Calvin Schermerhorn,** *The Business of Slavery and the Rise of American Capitalism, 1815-1860* (New Haven: Yale University Press, 2015)

Southern bankers, in moves that have been repeated in today's society, created financial instruments wherein loans for the purchase of slaves were mortgaged. The mortgages---securities, really---were sliced into sellable units and sold in securities markets in New York, London, and elsewhere in Europe. The European investors wanted protection for their loans, so the financiers were able to get state governments to provide guarantees in the event the slaveholding borrowers defaulted on their mortgages. Basically, the public was responsible for the government guarantees that would secure the interests of New York and European investors in the slave trade. "Slavery's bankers" made the expansion of the slave market a reality from 1820 to 1860.

Sounds suspiciously like the mortgage market in the early 2000s, doesn't it?

The South's economy was overwhelmingly agricultural, which required land. The original inhabitants of the best agricultural areas (Florida, Georgia, Alabama, Arkansas, Louisiana, and South Carolina) at the time were Seminoles, Cherokees, Creeks, Choctaws, and Chickasaws. A slaveholding plantation owner from Tennessee, our 7th President, Andrew Jackson, acceded to the demands of large-scale Southern property owners, as well as other land grabbers, and initiated the *Indian Removal Act*, which he signed on May 28, 1830. This Act resulted in many thousands of Indians being forced from their homes and relocated to the West, on what became known as the Trail of Tears.

The broken promises of the government, the theft of land, the destruction of culturally-significant areas, all showed the Native Americans that the white man valued land more than lives, and had no regard for the Indians' histories or cultures. This was a bitter pill for them to swallow, because it was based on profound differences in values. Whites thought that they could "own" land, whereas, Indians thought that they were only stewards of the Earth, entrusted with its careful use for the sake of generations to come.

The horrors of slavery took place at the same time. From about 1525 to 1866, first the Spanish, then the colonies and states, were responsible for importing about 388,000 slaves directly to North

America, although a total of about 10.7 million slaves were brought to the Caribbean and South America in the same time[27].

The cruelties perpetrated against the slaves and their families are the subject of studies and discussions elsewhere. Suffice it to say that many Northerners (and some Southerners) were opposed to slavery on moral and religious grounds. They felt that it degraded the slave owners in God's eyes, and betrayed the religious values supposedly shared by everyone. The Abolitionists believed that there was a moral imperative to abolish slavery and create better living conditions for the blacks. Some argued that free labor was more effective than slave labor and on economic grounds believed in freedom as being good for the economy.

Eventually, the Civil War erupted. Over four years, nearly 640,000 Americans fought and died. President Lincoln issued an Executive Order in January 1863 called the Emancipation Proclamation, freeing

---

[27] Henry Louis Gates, Jr., *The African-Americans: Many Rivers to Cross* (Kunhardt McGee Productions, THIRTEEN Productions LLC, Inkwell Films, in association with Ark Media, 2013)

the slaves. However, the 13th Amendment became the Constitutional basis for freeing the slaves throughout the entire United States, and it went into effect in December 1865.

After the Civil War, Southern landowners, especially plantation owners, no longer had slave labor to work the fields. A system of farming, sharecropping, was instituted in the South. The former slaves were given parcels of land to farm, often with seeds, tools, and farm animals loaned to the farmers, and with an agreement to share a portion of the proceeds with the land owner or the "plantation store." Using tricky legal agreements and/or high credit costs to keep the sharecroppers tied to the land, the land owners took advantage of the illiteracy of many blacks. Essentially, the sharecroppers were operating like feudal serfs on the estates (plantations) on which they were former slaves, and could not leave.

Starting in the 1870s, impoverished white farmers in the South, ravished by the losses caused by the Civil War, likewise had little choice but to become sharecroppers. Over the next 60 years, sharecropping throughout the South was bi-racial. Given the legacy of slavery in the South, white sharecroppers automatically assumed that they were "superior" to their black fellow sharecroppers, and Southern legislators perpetrated a gradated compensation scale wherein black farmers earned less than their white counterparts.

The system of racism-tainted sharecropping lasted up until the eve of World War II, when mechanical processes and improved tools made sharecropping a disappearing part of the Southern landscape.

As World War II pulled more and more white men into the military, increasing numbers of blacks moved north to Chicago, Detroit, Cincinnati, Akron, Youngstown, Pittsburgh, and other places where the demands of the war required able hands to work in the factories, shipyards, and supply depots. Blacks rapidly learned industrial skills; improved their abilities to communicate; got better pay than in the rural/agricultural South; and became exposed to city life. However, due to the widespread Jim Crow laws, blacks still suffered from the effects of legally-sanctioned segregation, with separate (and inferior) facilities such as restrooms, drinking fountains, dining areas, schools, transportation accommodations, shopping, and housing.

Black men also joined the armed forces, but were still racially segregated. It wasn't until July 1948 that President Harry S. Truman finally desegregated the military by issuing an Executive Order.

In the late 1940s and early '50s, most blacks felt that they had more than earned their right to be treated equally, having fought and served bravely in World War II. They came home, only to be treated as second-class citizens, without dignity or the freedom for which they had fought. This unfair treatment was still legal because the law of the land was based on the infamous "separate but equal" holding in the Supreme Court case, ***Plessy v. Ferguson***[28].

Groups such as the NAACP Legal Defense Committee fought to end the legal forms of segregation and brought the famous case of ***Brown v. Board of Education of Topeka***[29] to the U.S. Supreme Court. In that case, the Supreme Court explicitly overturned its earlier decision in ***Plessy v. Ferguson***, holding that legislatively-based segregation in education was unconstitutional.

After ***Brown v. Board of Education***, the Civil Rights movement began to develop momentum. When Rosa Parks, an African-American woman, refused to give up her seat to a white man in the "whites-only" section of a city bus in Montgomery, Alabama in 1955, her protest triggered numerous marches, rallies, and civil disobedience campaigns by people such as Dr. Martin Luther King, Jr. and Ralph Abernathy. In particular, Dr. King's leadership of the Civil Rights cause triggered a powerful series of changes in America.

In 1964, President Lyndon B. Johnson pushed Congress aggressively for civil rights legislation, and they passed the Civil Rights Act of 1964. A year later, Congress passed the Voting Rights Act of 1965, which ended official, *de jure* restrictions on voting in federal, state, and local elections.

However, *de facto* segregation continued, in housing, schooling, and governmental representation. Banks engaged in widespread lending violations based on "redlining," illegal restrictions or denials of lending because people lived in areas deemed to represent poor

---

[28] *Plessy v. Ferguson* (1896) 163 U.S. 537
[29] *Brown v. Board of Education of Topeka* (1954) 347 U.S. 483

financial risk. Schools in minority areas received far less financial support than schools in predominantly white areas. Government services were poorly distributed to those in poor, i.e., African-American, areas, and it was hard to elect non-white people to city, county or state government offices.

Discrimination in these areas, as well as jobs, were all based on racism in one way or another, and blacks often felt that the deck was stacked against them.

Long-simmering frustration with the systematized racism throughout the country finally led to riots in Los Angeles, Detroit, Newark, New York, Baltimore, Cleveland, San Francisco, Birmingham, Milwaukee, Philadelphia, and many other places in the 1960s.

On top of everything else, young people were being drafted to go to war in Vietnam. Women were starting to seek their own civil rights. And even gays in New York started a new movement for equality and an end to bias based on sexual orientation.

In short, the 1960s was a cauldron of dramatic social changes, and it was the accumulation of these changes that altered our economy.

The economy of this country reflected the state of social and political conditions. For most of our history before and after the Revolution, America was an agricultural society. However, World War II required a radical transformation of our economic base, and it became clear that we had to accelerate our move into manufacturing and improve all the systems to modernize the work flow so the factories would run efficiently.

Changes had been made as the result of the Great Depression---banking; insurance; electrification; improvements in the highways, bridges, and ports; telephones; air travel; and many other areas that we would recognize as the foundation of modern life. The war sped up that process of change.

Within a year after the end of the Second World War, Britain's Prime Minister, Winston Churchill, had made his famous speech at a college in Fulton, Missouri. In it, he declared, in part: "From Stettin in the Baltic to Trieste in the Adriatic, an iron curtain has descended across the Continent."

It was that "Iron Curtain" speech which launched the Cold War and established bitter enmity between the then-Soviet Union and America until the falling of the Berlin Wall in 1989.

During that 43-year period, America's economy transformed itself into a post-war behemoth. Due to its fortunate location between the Atlantic and the Pacific Oceans, America was highly unlikely to suffer from mass invasions, unlike those countries in Europe and in the Far East which had suffered from military invasions and their concomitant warfare. America lost significant numbers of military personnel in the European, African, and Pacific Theaters of World War II, but their 419,000 total losses were not remotely close to the nearly 27 **million** Soviet people killed during World War II in all parts of the Soviet Union.

The American economy was so strong in the aftermath of the war that it chose to implement a number of programs to help restore former enemies, such as the Japanese, the Italians, and the Germans, to a position of relative economic strength so as to avoid creating post-war conditions like those that prevailed after World War I and which led to the great catastrophe of the Second World War. Programs such as the Marshall Plan to help Western Europe, and the occupation and restoration of the Japanese islands and their economy by General Douglas A. MacArthur from 1945 - 1952 were wise moves on the part of the U.S. government.

America's economy during World War II was militarized, as was its political structure. There was respect for the leaders in Congress, many of whom had served during the War. Communications were subject to scrutiny ("loose lips sink ships") and there was widespread trust in authority. Bi-partisanship was widespread in both Congress and on the state level.

As the military service personnel returned home, most got married, and that began what would be known as the "Baby Boom" generation. Soldiers, sailors, and airmen were provided with free education under the G.I. Montgomery Bill. Suddenly, a generation of young people were being educated; homes were being built everywhere; expansion of manufacturing plants took place overnight; and whole industries were being created to take care of the needs of the growing suburban families. Baby food, toys, clothing; schools and homes; cars and fast food; television; popular culture; all were being modernized and expanded as the generation that overcame the evil of war settled down and raised families.

The Right Wingers Can't Fight Fair, So They Fight Foul

In some respects, the 1950s was viewed as a sedate decade if you were part of the white middle class and had a good job. If you were black or brown, of course, life wasn't so good, because there was a tremendous gap between the whites and the non-whites. Black and brown people generally led much better lives after the War than before, but it was even more cruel to see that white ex-soldiers/sailors were doing so well while their black and brown countrymen were falling farther and farther behind.

That economic disparity was bad, but the lack of social dignity and respect was particularly hard to bear. Black and brown soldiers, sailors, and airmen had done their part in Europe and in the Pacific, but were not given the same victory parades or treated with the same respect as their white counterparts.

Thus, the Civil Rights movement had multiple parts to it: social justice; economic justice; and voting justice. The blacks and browns had done their part to "save the American pie." Now, they thought it only fair that they be given a piece, too.

Minority cries for justice were subject to the distractions of the "Red Scare" during the late 1940s through the 1950s. The national paranoia and fear in America, arising from the Cold War, led most papers, magazines, radio, and television news reports to concentrate on the perceived threats from the Soviet Union. Our own domestic troubles were left on the sidelines while we tried to figure out what to do about the Soviets.

With Wisconsin Senator Joseph McCarthy's ascent to power, beginning in 1947, he used paranoia as an adjunct to the underlying bigotry against Jews that was widespread throughout America. The "Father of Hate Radio," Father Charles Coughlin, had been broadcasting on his "Hour of Power" show for years, telling his many listeners of the "evil misdeeds" of the "Children of Zion." His widely-heard hatemongering, coupled with Senator McCarthy's own rants, supported by the up-and-coming right-wingers such as Richard Nixon, created a *Zeitgeist* of fear and a desire to return to America's pre-War isolationism without being troubled with and by foreign threats.

At about the same time, starting in 1947, the House Un-American Activities Committee began investigating allegations of Communist influence and subversion in the U.S. during the early years of the Cold War. Committee members quickly focused their investigations on the Hollywood film industry, which they viewed as a hotbed of communist activity. This reputation originated in the 1930s, when the economic difficulties of the Great Depression increased the appeal of leftist organizations for many struggling actors and studio workers.

During the next several years, HUAC continued its witch hunt, and the result was that many of America's most talented writers, actors, directors, and producers were fired by the studios. The leaders of this group, known as the "Hollywood 10," paid a deep price, with fines and jail time, not to mention loss of income and social ostracism. It so happened that many of the actors, writers, and other members of the film industry were Jewish. Their identities were disclosed, and their Jewishness exacerbated the already-existing anti-Semitism throughout the country.

The "Red Scare" era was full of fear-mongering in the press. The Russians had exploded a nuclear bomb in 1949; the Chinese Communists had taken over mainland China the same year; and in 1950 the Russians supported the North Koreans, who invaded South Korea, leading to the Korean War.

Rumors persisted about an "international Jewish conspiracy," and fuel was put on that fire when it was learned that Klaus Fuchs (the German-born British scientist who closely participated with us on the "Manhattan Project" and who gave our atomic secrets to the Russians) worked with Harry Gold (the English middleman between Fuchs and the Soviets). When Gold was arrested, he was connected to David Greenglass, which led to the arrest of his sister-in-law, Ethel Rosenberg, and her husband Julius Rosenberg. Right-wingers throughout the country noted that Gold, Greenglass, and the

Rosenbergs were all Jewish, and that triggered many virulent, anti-Semitic rants in the media.

HUAC and McCarthy continued their investigations and accusations. McCarthy became more and more incensed about his so-called "evidence" of State Dept. infiltration by communists. His accusations were not supported by facts, but that was of no import to him. He would wave blank pieces of paper at his desk in the Senate, and make wild assertions about the increasing number of communists in the State Dept. and elsewhere in the government.

What brought McCarthy down was his incendiary claim about communists infiltrating the U.S. Army. During televised hearings against the Army, he mercilessly attacked a young lawyer named Fred Fisher, making reckless and untrue accusations about his loyalties. The Army's Chief Counsel, Joseph Welch, thundered back at McCarthy: "Have you no decency, sir, at long last? Have you left no sense of decency?" Most Americans, seeing this, were disgusted with McCarthy. The Republican leadership, understanding what a liability he had become, censured him.

Not long afterwards, McCarthy was gone from the Senate, and he died in May 1957.

Continuing with the country's anti-Jewish sentiments, in December 1958, the John Birch Society was founded in Indianapolis, Indiana. It was (and to this day is) an ultra-right-wing conservative group, which has been staunchly anti-communist for the last 60 years. It can truthfully be said to be the ideological precursor to the Tea Party, evangelicals, and alt-right movements over the last couple of decades. It strongly urged people to listen to its anti-Semitic and anti-communist rants, and its publications were the forefathers of The Breitbart News Network and The Fox News Network.

With the ferment going on in this country in the post-WWII period, America's ideological orientation was being skewed from one end of the economic spectrum to the other. But what was fundamental and unchanging was the militarization of our economy.

During World War II, it was necessary for the United States to make every effort to modernize its economy, especially its production lines. Tanks, planes, ships, trucks, jeeps, guns, ammunition, radios, every mechanical and electrical device needed for the military had to be produced in record time. As a matter of survival, we deemed it vital to our national self-defense that we militarize our economy.

Everything was subordinated to the demands of production. Therefore, we developed new systems of organization; purchasing; communications; distribution; and strategic planning. These tools led to a strong, unyielding alliance between the military and industry. This bond became too close after the war, and led to President Dwight Eisenhower warning us of the dangers of the Military-Industrial Complex ("MIC") in his farewell speech to the nation at the end of his second term.

Between 1950 and 1989, the Cold War divided the world into two factions: the Soviet Bloc and the Western Bloc. Accusations of "Western Imperialism" were met by equally-strong allegations of "Communist infiltration" everywhere. The result was a world full of conflicted interests that did not provide people with an honest, neutral view of how we could improve the economy to make each society a better one. The "Communist threat," manifested in the Warsaw Pact countries' alliance with the Soviet Union, meant that there were large parts of Europe that were no longer friendly with the United States. Conversely, the NATO countries were inextricably-opposed to cooperating with Russia and its allies.

The result was that for much of the world, the so-called Third World, people sided with one power or another. Shrewd government leaders in the developing countries across the globe exploited the ideological differences between East and West. They made (or pretended to make) alliances with the Soviets against the U.S. in order to get financial aid and military support. The same principle held true where many countries sided with the U.S. against the Soviets.

Both groups of Third World nations wound up playing off the two super powers against each other like children do with parents who are in the midst of a divorce.

The pro-American and pro-Soviet hostility created huge arms'-race programs in the U.S.S.R. and in the U.S. Our expenditures for military items amounted to hundreds of billions of dollars per year, and far exceeded the outlays made by the Soviets and their associates.

With American arrogance, we claimed to be the world's policeman. With that self-appointed title, we took it upon ourselves to provide foreign aid to any government who would buy weapons from us. We had huge sectors of our economy tied up with defense spending, whether it was electronics; vehicles (sea, land, air); missiles and related armaments; chemical and atomic weapons. Transportation; communications; computers; electronics; and many other areas were directly or indirectly participating in our arms'-race based economy. Even the so-called Space Race was directly attributable to the launching of Sputnik 1 by the Soviets in 1957. (John Kennedy's speech about going to the moon wasn't a precursor to Star Trek; it was a desire to play tit-for-tit against the Soviets, who put the first artificial earth satellite into orbit.)

It would be more than fair to refer to government policy towards the MIC as "socialism for the corporations." Conversely, capitalism is consigned to the poor and struggling lower middle class. This description is based on facts, those being:

1. Tax policies and procedures favor corporations over individuals (corporations have lower tax rates, more legal deductions, chances to move money off-shore in ways that are almost impossible for individuals to achieve, protection for shareholders that are not available to sole proprietors, and handouts to the MIC through pork barrel legislation which benefits both the recipients of pork barrel spending and the Congressmen/-women and/or Senators who shepherd the bill through Congress). Pork barrel spending winds up costing taxpayers far more money because of the high profits typically associated with given projects. The MIC profits from waste, and there is no meaningful way at present to accurately account for, or even properly audit, what all our military money buys. There are a few poster-children for MIC waste: $640 for a toilet seat; $7,600 for a coffee pot; a gear worth $500 that was paid for by the Pentagon at $8,000, etc.[30]

---

[30] William D. Hartung, *Only the Pentagon Could Spend $640 on a Toilet Seat* (<u>The Nation</u>, April 11, 2016)

2. The MIC typically will set up plants or other facilities in as many states as possible. In that way, when they come to Congress looking for money, they will say that "If we don't get 'X' billions of dollars for this program, 50,000 jobs will be lost." No Congressperson or Senator wants to go back to his/her constituents and say "I voted 'No" on Such-and-Such Corporation's request for funds."

3. The corporations have long received legislative favors from Congress as the result of their campaign contributions. Their interests have typically been expressed through the offices of lobbyists in Washington, DC. Individuals generally don't enjoy the access to lobbyists, unless those individuals are at least deca-millionaires.

So those facts strongly support the notion that we spend hundreds of billions of dollars per year paying for the American military, yet have no clear idea of what we're getting for our money. And when it comes to the non-military corporations, the same tax and other laws that benefit the MIC also confer advantages on their non-military counterparts.

The result of this legislative bias in favor of corporations is the decline in American infrastructure, health care, education, communications, media, environmental protection, and research and development.

In short, our economy was initially agricultural and was very largely supported by slavery and the theft of land and resources from the Native Americans. Secondly, the advent of World War II made it necessary to militarize the economy. The wartime need for that militarization ended in 1945, but for the last 75 years we have engaged in feeding the hungry maw of the MIC. This domination of our economy by the MIC and corporate interests has led to significant decline in America, stemming from fundamental policy miscues:

1. We have become enslaved by the MIC.

2. Our Internal Revenue tax rates have dramatically declined over the last two generations, and the recent tax cut bill which passed through Congress in December 2017 has created a path towards economic hell if we don't reverse it soon.

3. Tariffs need to be adjusted so that trade relations create mutual benefit. We gave away the store back in the 1970s, and need to adjust the rates appropriately.

4. We have virtually stopped the role of government in helping to provide low-cost/no-cost loans and/or grants to small businesses, which are the job creators in this country.

5. We allow corporate and securities laws to have changed so that the pay-gap between the founder/owners of the business and the lowest-paid workers is appallingly high. This dramatically reduces productivity and lowers prospects for long-range growth of a sustainable economy. As noted by President Barack Obama in his December 4, 2013 "Inequality Speech" at Town Hall Education Arts Recreations Campus in Washington, D.C.:

"And the result is an economy that's become profoundly unequal, and families that are more insecure. I'll just give you a few statistics. Since 1979, when I graduated from high school, our productivity is up by more than 90 percent, but the income of the typical family has increased by less than eight percent. Since 1979, our economy has more than doubled in size, but most of that growth has flowed to a fortunate few.

"The top 10 percent no longer takes in one-third of our income -- it now takes half. Whereas in the past, the average CEO made about 20 to 30 times the income of the average worker, today's CEO now makes 273 times more. And meanwhile, a family in the top 1 percent has a net worth 288 times higher than the typical family, which is a record for this country."

What Can be Done to Right These Wrongs?

In the next chapters, we'll explore proposals to help address the problems deriving from defective income streams, gross incompetence in budgeting/accounting/auditing the military, and ways to get America to the point where it should be, for its own citizens, residents, and countries around the world.

CHAPTER 14
FREEDOM FROM THE MILITARY-INDUSTRIAL COMPLEX

The history of mankind is rife with illustrations of the use of military force as an ingredient of political influence. Battles and bloodshed have frequently preceded regime changes, the creation of new alliances or the destruction of old, the creation or destruction of city-states and their successors. The ancient wars on foot and horseback, with spears, swords, bows and arrows, have been replaced by modern warfare, with machine guns, jets, tanks, missiles, ships, and countless other armaments. But the underlying motivations---greed, lust for glory, acquisition of new territories, gaining trade routes or partners---have not changed.

The same principle applied to the development and use of military force in the United States from pre-Revolutionary times to the present. With us, we have seemed to need external justifications for deploying force overseas, since we were fortunately situated with two large oceans flanking us, making massive armed invasions extremely difficult to mobilize and maintain.

Nonetheless, during World War II, it became clear that American military help was essential in defeating Nazi Germany and Imperial Japan. The threats posed by both powers to our allies and what we considered to be American interests made isolationism a non-starter. After the bombing of Pearl Harbor, Hawai'i on December 7, 1941 and our colony, the Philippines, on December 8, it was clear that American interests required an armed response.

There was also the serious problem of the attacks on Great Britain, and the capture of France and other countries in Europe. From September 1, 1939 (the Nazi invasion of Poland) up through 1942, Nazi Germany appeared to be invincible, and it appeared their U-boats could potentially devastate our naval forces, making an invasion possible. The Japanese were likewise threatening, and their forcing of General Douglas MacArthur to abandon the Philippines and his decision to withdraw to Australia was a great shock to the American military and political leadership.

Thus, in the face of the twin threats from Germany and Japan, the U.S. was under a real military threat for the first time in its existence. In the period from 1942 to 1945, the U.S. armaments industry came to dominate life in America. Everything associated with defense was given top priority. Blacks were drawn from the South to defense factories in the North. Females were likewise given the opportunity to work on factory lines. Civilians sacrificed purchases of automobiles, appliances, personal attire, all for the sake of making resources available for our fighting forces overseas. Communities throughout the country ran scrap-metal collection drives; blood drives; and especially joined together to buy war bonds. The U.S. budget showed defense spending of about 2% of GDP in the 1930s; during WW II, our defense budget increased to 41% of GDP[31].

Shortly after the end of WW II, the Soviet Union and America divided the world into two ideological blocks. The genuine fear of the Nazis and the Japanese military that prevailed during the War was immediately replaced by a national paranoia based on fears of "the Red Menace." Propaganda in the news, radio shows, magazines, and public speeches trumpeted notions of the communist threat to America. Politicians and committees in Congress made spectacular (and false) accusations about the Soviets and the influence the communist party had in the State Department, the Army, and the movie industry.

As was discussed in the preceding chapter, the United States was locked into a military mindset during WW II as a matter of necessity, but afterwards we were brainwashed into thinking that the "evil Soviets" were bent on world domination. Our paranoia grew after former British Prime Minister Winston Churchill gave his "Iron Curtain" speech in Fulton, Missouri, on March 5, 1946, launching the

---

[31] Usgovernmentspending.com

start of the Cold War, and warning the world that the Soviet Union intended to continue its expansion throughout Europe.

Speaking while U.S. President Harry S. Truman was seated on the platform, Churchill condemned the "communist fifth columns" operating in western and southern Europe, and drew parallels with the former Prime Minister Neville Chamberlain's disastrous policy of appeasing Hitler before the War. Churchill called for a strengthening of the "special relationship" between Great Britain and America, characterizing them as the "great powers of the English-speaking world," and said that they, alone, should organize and police the postwar world.

(American military and government personnel were not entirely convinced that it was wise to hitch America's wagon to England's star; Great Britain was in decline, and our officials did not want to be used as pawns in supporting the crumbling British Empire.)

In his speech, Churchill strongly noted that in dealing with the Soviets there was "nothing which they admire so much as strength, and there is nothing for which they have less respect than for military weakness."

Shortly after the speech, a civil war broke out in Greece (1946 - 1949), with fighting between the communist ELAS group and Greece's army. The army, supported by the U.K. and the U.S., fought against communist rebels supported by Yugoslavia, Albania, and Bulgaria. Of significance was the fact that Joseph Stalin opposed the civil war, but ELAS was greatly helped by Yugoslavia's Marshal Josip Broz Tito[32]. This was the first proxy war between East and West.

In the U.S., there was not much accurate reporting of the Greek Civil War, and what news there was made it seem to most Americans that this was just a kind of nuisance fighting in the Aegean Sea between the Greeks and some "troublemakers." What reporting there was made it seem as though the war was stimulated by Joseph Stalin and the Soviets. In looking at declassified papers, it turns out that Stalin opposed the war, whereas it was Yugoslavia's leader, Josep

---

[32] Mogens Pelt, *Tying Greece to the West: US-West German-Greek Relations 1949-1974*, p. 129 (<u>Museum Tusculanum Press</u>, 2006)

Broz Tito, who supported the communists in their fight against the government. This reflected the Stalin-Tito split of 1948[33].

A year after Churchill's speech, President Truman issued the "Truman Doctrine," which was his foreign policy principle geared towards containing Soviet geopolitical expansion.

The years 1947-1949 were strange for postwar Americans. On the one hand, former soldiers and sailors returned to peaceful conditions at home; many got educations, obtained jobs, and formed families. Factories converted their manufacturing from tanks to toasters, airplanes to automobiles, and radar to refrigerators. New industries began to spring up to accommodate the needs of America's booming population of growing families. Things appeared to be settling down, and in some quarters there were strong calls for disarmament.

But then, the Soviet Union and its allies dramatically expanded their own military capabilities, and moved into the atomic age. By 1949, the Soviet Union had detonated its first atomic bomb, and made clear that it was not going to play second fiddle to the United States or its allies.

With Churchill's warnings ringing in our ears; with the Greek Civil War in our news broadcasts; with radio commentators issuing philippics against the Soviets every day and night, the American public felt that it had just survived one terrible nightmare only to find itself immersed in another.

Right after Japan surrendered in World War II, Indonesia declared its independence from the Netherlands. Americans lost their Southeast Asian colony, the Philippines, in 1946. Britain experienced losses in its empire, too: Jordan in 1946; India and Pakistan in 1947; Burma, Ceylon, and Israel in 1948. Korean was divided into North and South Korea in 1948, and the People's Republic of China was formed in 1949.

Overwhelmed by the sudden, dramatic postwar changes, our Congress and other branches of government, our religious institutions,

---

[33] Jordan Baev, *The Greek Civil War Viewed From the North* (paper presented at an International Conference in April 1999 at King's College, London.)

our news, all broadcast the dangers of the Cold War and the arm's race born from the ideological conflicts between East and West. It seemed uncertainty was everywhere, and it was hard to predict what would come next. At this point, America's short-lived affair with disarmament was clearly over, and it became the focal point of our government's policies to reaffirm the military's ties to industry.

The Korean War in 1950 further tightened the bonds between the American military and industry. Whereas in World War II, we mostly looked to improve production of existing technologies, the Korean War saw new technologies being advanced: jets, improved tanks, better missiles, more electronic weapons. The Russians were using this conflict to show the West that they were no slouches when it came to armaments. America felt it had no choice but to up the ante when it came to weaponry.

Britain and America joined forces during the 1950s and '60s to fight against Soviet influence. After its catastrophic losses during World War II, the Soviets made it clear that they would never falter in the arms race. They spent great portions of their resources in developing new weapons systems that would prevent them from being subordinate to the West. From armaments research came new planes, missiles, bombs, electronics, computers, ships and submarines, with increasingly sophisticated methods of training their troops in advanced warfare tactics. From a strategic perspective, the Soviets used their Warsaw Pact client-states as buffers to deter Western aggression.

English political prevarication has a long and infamous history, and the United Kingdom convinced the Americans---the Brits' protégés in the field of deception---to join it in countering the efforts of the Soviets and their allies in asserting dominance in Europe and elsewhere, and in protecting British and U.S. interests. As a result, in 1950, Iranian prime minister, Mohammed Mossadegh, attracted the ire of Britain by nationalizing the British-owned Anglo-Iranian Oil Company; by 1953, Dr. Mossadegh was ousted in a coup sponsored by the U.K. and U.S. intelligence services. The Shah of Iran, Mohammad Reza Pahlavi, came to power. Not long thereafter, the

CIA was brought in by the Shah to form his secret police, known as "SAVAK."

SAVAK was notoriously brutal and engaged in kidnappings, detentions, torture, and executions of anyone remotely suspected of threatening or challenging the Shah's regime. It was, essentially, the Persian version of the Nazis' *Gestapo*. It was tragically ironic that it was created by many of the same U.S. intelligence personnel who had cut their foreign-affairs eyeteeth on fighting the Nazis[34].

The Persians, a proud people with a long and storied history, did not happily live under the brutal hand of the Shah, nor by being subservient to a dictatorship; they bitterly chafed at the Pahlavi regime's repression. Finally, in 1979, they revolted and staged an overthrow of the Shah, instituting a popular conversion from a 2,500 year-long monarchy to an Islamist Republic led by the Ayatollah Ruhollah Khomeini.

Before this, during the 1950s through April 1975, the United States had been involved in the military conflict in Vietnam. Even before we entered into the Korean War, in 1950 the U.S. sent military advisors to Vietnam (then called French Indochina, reflecting its colonial status)[35]. The French, trying to hold onto the last of their Far East empire, struggled against the Viet Cong at Dien Bien Phu in April 1954. They lost the battle, and their Asian empire. Interestingly, the U.S. paid for most of the French war effort.[36]

America's hidden support of the French was based on the efforts of several of its key government hawks: Vice President Richard Nixon; Admiral Arthur W. Radford, Chairman of the Joint Chiefs of Staff; and the US Secretary of State, John Foster Dulles, who was obsessed

---

[34] M. J. Gasiorowski, Nikkie R. Keddie, eds., *Neither East Nor West: Iran, the Soviet Union, and the United States*, pp. 148–51 (New Haven: Yale University Press, 1990)

[35] Major General George S. Eckhardt, *Vietnam Studies Command and Control 1950-1969*, p. 6 (Department of the Army, Washington, D.C., 1991)

[36] *Dien Bien Phu: Did the US offer France an A-bomb?* (BBC News Magazine, May 5, 2014)

by the crusade against Communism (as was his brother, Allen Dulles, the Director of the CIA).

The rationalization for our involvement in this fight was the so-called "Domino Theory," articulated by President Eisenhower at a press conference in early April 1954 as describing the possible spread of Communism from one country to another: "You have a row of dominoes set up, you knock over the first one, and what will happen to the last one is the certainty that it will go over very quickly," he said. "So you could have a beginning of a disintegration that would have the most profound influences."[37]

The Domino Theory was heavily endued in American foreign policy by Presidents Eisenhower, Kennedy, and Johnson as the basis for providing economic and military assistance to the South Vietnamese. In adherence to this theory, the U.S. escalated its military involvement in Vietnam starting in the early 1960s, tripling the size of its troop deployment in 1961 and tripling it again in 1962. In addition to the Special Forces (Green Berets), in 1965 the U.S. authorized the deployment of regular ground forces.

The Vietnam War was a disaster for countless civilians living in South and North Vietnam, as well as Cambodia and Laos, bordering countries where the North Vietnamese forces (the Viet Cong) stored supplies and from which they launched attacks against the U.S. and its allies. It was the biggest proxy war of the Cold War era. The North Vietnamese were supported by the Soviet Union, China, Cuba, North Korea, the Khmer Rouge, and the Pathet Lao, while the South Vietnamese were backed by the United States, South Korea, Thailand, Australia, New Zealand, the Khmer Republic, the Kingdom of Laos, and Taiwan. Estimates of Vietnamese casualties varied, with the largest number being 3.1 million soldiers and civilians. The U.S. lost 58,200 armed personnel, with over 1,600 missing in action.[38]

---

[37] Presidential response to question by reporter Robert Richards, <u>Copley Press</u>, April 7, 1954

[38] Obermeyer, Ziad; Murray, Christopher J.L.; Gakidou, Emmanuela, *Fifty Years of Violent War Deaths From Vietnam to*

During the Vietnam War, our MIC had the greenlight to manufacture new technologies or to make improvements to existing technologies. Jets, armaments, ships, pesticides/defoliants, helicopters, bombs, electronics, guns, were all the subject of high-scale/high-cost procurements which added billions of dollars of profits to American arms manufacturers.[39]

Now, we have to ask ourselves, in the 45 years since Americans left the Vietnam War, what did our anti-communism bring us?

Here's a brief inventory of the results of our anti-communism crusade:

The end of the Shah's regime; the Russian Afghan War (where we funded the *mujahideen* under Osama bin Laden, in opposition to the Russians); the Lebanese Civil War; our invasion of Grenada; our support of the *contras* (right-wing guerrillas in Nicaragua); the first Persian Gulf War in 1991; the rise of Al-Qaeda, founded by Osama bin Laden; the rise of the Taliban in Afghanistan; the attack on our World Trade Center in New York; the second Gulf War in Iraq and a separate war in Afghanistan.

In that time, there came an end to the Cold War, with the agreement between Russian President Mikhail Gorbachev and U.S. President George H.W. Bush in December 1989 to put an end to their countries' geopolitical rivalries, and to work more closely together in what Pres. Bush later called a "New World Order."[40]

Sadly, however, we got rid of one "ogre" (the Soviet Union and its Communist ideology) only to replace it with another one (the "War on Terror").

During the Cold War, the United States spent trillions of dollars arming themselves for a direct confrontation with the Soviet Union that fortunately never came. Regardless, thousands of American lives

---

Bosnia: Analysis of Data from the World Health Survey Programme, pp. 1482-1486 (BMJ. 2008)

[39] History.com staff, *Weapons of the Vietnam War*, 2011

[40] BBC Home, *1989: Malta Summit Ends Cold War*, December 3, 1989

were lost waging proxy wars in Korea and Vietnam. (*The Reagan Years: the End of the Cold War*[41] UShistory.org/us/59e.asp)

Sed quis custodiet ipsos custodes (But who shall guard the guardians?) - Juvenal

---

Despite the lack of objective, forensically-verifiable evidence of military threats from Russia, we still are enthralled by the MIC. We're budgeting so much money for the MIC, not to mention the off-balance sheet expenditures for the intelligence agencies. All of this is tied into the notion that a militarized economy is good for the U.S., and is necessary for the rest of the world.

However, one wonders whether this is so. In 2011, the U.S. spent more on its military ($711 billion) than the next 13 nations combined ($695 billion)[42]. In 2019, Pres. Trump has proposed a budget for the military of over $718 billion, plus another $200 billion for off-balance sheet expenditures.

---

[41] *The Reagan Years: the End of the Cold War*, UShistory.org/us/59e.asp

[42] Brad Plumer, *America's Staggering Defense Budget, in Charts* (<u>The Washington Post</u>, January 7, 2013)

When Trump campaigned for the Presidency, he criticized foreign trade agreements he called "terrible, absolute disasters" (NAFTA, the proposed American participation in the Trans-Pacific Partnership; and others). He thought it important to make major cuts in domestic spending, but to add another 10% to the Pentagon's budget. Apparently, Trump's desire to "Make America Great Again" is reflected substantially in having an enhanced military with all the additional equipment that an enhanced military requires[43].

The costs associated with the MIC are not limited to the direct costs of weaponry. It should be remembered that defense contractors (and their civilian counterparts) enter into bidding wars where various municipalities compete to have these businesses set up in their communities. This typically involves getting extended income tax holidays; often the donation of the land on which to build a factory; "...and sometimes the cost of building and equipping the factory itself at taxpayers' expense. Cities and towns are that eager to have a factory, with its network of nearby suppliers and its relatively well-paying jobs — relative, that is, to the lower paying retail and service industry work that is often the alternative for high-school- or even junior-college-educated men and women."[44]

These bids often cost a community up to $100 million for the "privilege" of having a business locate there.[45]

Beyond weapons costs, there is an entirely new component added to the MIC: cyber intelligence. In addition to human spying and analysis, there are many technological aspects, with new computer systems, networks, spying gear, data farms, satellites, communication systems, and additional nodes in our array of intelligence-gathering tools.

---

[43] Louis Uchitell, *The U.S. Still Leans on the Military-Industrial Complex* (The New York Times, September 22, 2017)

[44] *Id.*

[45] *Id.*

But more significantly, after September 11, the entire MIC in the U.S. became completely fixated on security. Building on the USA PATRIOT ACT, establishing the Dept. of Homeland Security, creating multiple new or enhanced intelligence services, the number of personnel now working in the American security industry is high. In fact, "...there are now 854,000 contract personnel with top-secret clearances — a number greater than that of top-secret-cleared civilian employees of the government."[46]

The contract personnel are composed of analysts, computer programmers, security system and network administrators, communications specialists, and many others whose work is buried deep within the security apparatus.

The security industry---government and the Silicon Valley working in collusion---is the updated version of the MIC. The difference between the arms manufacturers and the computer industry is that the former sells to the government, while the latter confines its sales overwhelmingly to the private sector. However, the government needs what Silicon Valley offers, and so the two have developed a new relationship.

The computer industry has, for years, tracked what its users do, for commercial purposes; the government wants to be able to indulge its infinite demand to know what everyone is doing, "for security purposes." As Edward Snowden revealed about the National Security Agency, its reach is long and deep, but Congress had reacted strongly to the NSA's overreach, and then-President Obama had to come to terms with the public's outrage over the intrusions into their personal lives.[47]

As the Summer 2018 testimony of Facebook's Mark Zuckerberg before Congress demonstrated, people in this country are sick and tired of the government's, and the computer industry's, invasion of privacy. Perhaps the perceived violations of people's Fourth Amendment rights are not necessarily the only motivations against

---

[46] Mike Lofgren, *Essay: Anatomy of the Deep State* (Moyers & Company, BillMoyers.com, February 12, 2014)

[47] *Id.*

this new form of the MIC, but they certainly play an important role; hence, the raft of new "privacy policy" announcements by applications manufacturers, networks, and email companies.

So, what can be done to liberate ourselves from the old and/or new MIC?

- Public financing of elections to sever the artery of money between the corporate interests and financially dependent elected officials
- removal of the notion of "corporate free speech"
- prohibition of former government workers from becoming lobbyists (indeed, let us remove lobbyists)
- a tax policy that values human labor over financial manipulation
- a trade policy that favors exporting manufactured goods over exporting investment capital.

Once private money is taken out of public functions (elections, maintaining a government) it makes it much likelier that we can elect the type of political leaders who can benefit us, rather than the monied class.

We also must get rid of the idea that corporations are the same as natural persons. This notion was based on a misunderstanding of a Supreme Court case from 1886; and there is no true justification based on concepts of justice and fairness that would require this false equivalency.

Part of the process of "cleaning shop" is to remove the existence of lobbyists. There is no legitimate need for them.

Our tax codes need to be modified so that human labor is rewarded, while financial manipulation is not.

Finally, we can and must develop trade principles and policies that get back to the fundamental quality of creating value: selling something that is real and tangible, rather than allowing people to gain through shrewd investments in foreign countries that do not tax (or have much lower taxes) on the gains from our investment capital.

With these factors in place, along with the ones described in Chapter 1, we have a chance of building a free society that is not beholden to people who kill and/or spy for ill purposes.

CHAPTER 15
WANT A GOOD LIFE? INCREASE OUR TAX RATES.

This will not be a trip "down memory lane," giving people false notions of what life was like in Middle Class America in the 1950s---but it will cover some realities that are objectively verifiable. Compared to today's frenetic environment, the pace of life in the 1950s would have seemed idyllic. Without television on, hour after hour, day after day; without the Internet; without always-connected smart phones; in short, without all the means (or reasons) for being constantly in-touch (and distracted from being present in the "now"), people in the 1950s had dramatically different views of social relationships.

These relationships regulated peoples' life-destinies. Entire plot-lines, courses of action from adolescence to old age, were laid out by well-defined social boundaries. Where you born, raised, and educated largely determined how you would lead your life. In many respects, it was virtually impossible to escape from your background.

I was born in 1952, in Los Angeles, California. My parents were active members of a liberal church, the Unitarian-Universalist Church, here in L.A. It was a hotbed of radical activism, with members of the "Hollywood 10" frequently speaking there; rallies for civil rights efforts; anti-war efforts; pro-feminist efforts; etc. I was thus exposed, from a young age, to life in the "progressive lane" of early Baby Boom politics in L.A.

Of course, there were also openings in the social restraints generally prevalent in the late 1940s and early 1950s. There were many inventions, new ways of manufacturing, radical shifts in adjusting social and economic perspectives through advertising (mass marketing), all of which derived economic support from both businesses and government. And it took significant amounts of money to create those openings. New highways; automobile industry expansion; building entirely new communities in suburbia; electrification; telephone networks; computer and data networks, all were part of the public and private investments in infrastructure that redefined American life.

For its infrastructure programs, the government kept taxes high. People paid them. Things were built. People used them. Life was, generally, good.

From memory, I would say that life was substantially better in the 1950s than now---and there are numerous facts that support this position. These are:

1. Economic Growth and Less Debt

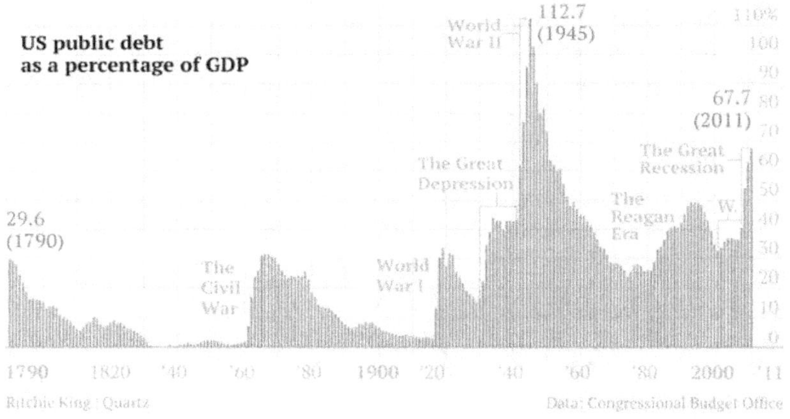

During the Great Depression, the U.S. unemployment rate was higher than 25%. In under two decades, in the 1950s, our unemployment rate was less than three per cent. Substantial parts of the population left the ranks of the impoverished and joined the Middle Class. By contrast, we have had, during 2008 - 2013, a jobless rate of about eight per cent. During the 1950s, a jobless person could get a new job in less than four months; today, it's about nine months---AND if you're older, your jobless status could last for well over two years. (National Bureau of Economic Research; BLS)

However, it's not just about much money you make, but how beholden you are to others. Debt is the great Slave Master of the American Economy, but it wasn't always that way. In 1950, Diner's Club issued a credit card, but its use was limited. In 1958, Bank of America issued a credit card, and the same year saw one issued by American Express Company, a so-called Travel and Entertainment Card, mostly used by traveling business executives and sales personnel.

By the 1960s, there was MasterCharge (later renamed to MasterCard), followed by Visa, Discover, and others. In the United States, these credit cards bore high interest rates and late fees; default charges; and other costs, many of which were not known to credit card users until they received their monthly statements. Over the years, the banks and credit card companies became enormously wealthy as the result of the imposition of so many hidden charges ("junk fees"), so much so that many people lobbied Congress for changes in the disclosure requirements pertaining to these cards. Finally, in April 2009, the House of Representatives approved the <u>Credit Card Holders' Bill of Rights</u>, which regulated and/or eliminated unfair and abusive credit card practices of the banks and credit card companies.

The Rule of 72

In America, the country with the highest amount of credit card debt, it was not at all uncommon to see annual interest rates of 24%. There is a rule about money that applies to both income and debt. It is called "The Rule of 72," and was a mathematical concept developed by Albert Einstein. He considered it to be his most important mathematical discovery, far more significant than "$E = mc^2$."

Interest is the Eighth Wonder of the World. He who understands it, earns it. He who doesn't, pays it. --- Albert Einstein

---

The Rule of 72 is based on a simple formula that allows a person to figure out how long it will take for their money to double in value. It works like this.

You invest a sum of money. You take the Return on Investment (ROI) and divide that number into 72. The result is the number of years it takes for your money to double. Here's an example. Imagine you have $10,000 to invest. You know you will get 6% annual ROI. Take 72, divide the ROI of 6% into it, and your $10,000 will double to $20,000 in 12 years. (72 / 6 = 12.)

The same principle applies to debt.

Suppose you have credit card debt of $10,000. The interest charged by your bank is 12%. At that rate, your $10,000 debt will double to $20,000 in six years. (72 / 12 = 6.)

It used to be that people could relatively easily file for bankruptcy protection and get rid of their consumer debt from credit cards. However, after intense lobbying by the banks and the Credit Card Association of America, Congress made a major revision to the Bankruptcy Act in 2005, which then-President George W. Bush signed in April of that year. The revised Bankruptcy Act made it much harder for people to escape from credit card debt (and also made it virtually impossible to get out of abusive student loans).

The result? People are enslaved by credit card debt, and their lack of self-discipline in some cases continues their bondage for years and years. However, because the cost of living has outstripped earning capacity for many years, and especially because the hyper-inflationary rate of medical expenses has outstripped virtually everything else in consumer/individual budgets, many people are paying for medical services through the use of their credit cards.

The average credit card debt per family in the U.S., as of 2017, is about $16,000, based on a recent study. In reality, this means that a family with income of $50,000 per year and the average amount of credit card debt is paying $904/year in card interest charges, and over $500/month in payments. (https://www.nerdwallet.com)

In the U.S., the average personal savings rate was 9.8% from 1950 through 2000. At its highest, it was 17% in May 1975 before beginning to decline[48].

Personal savings amounts have dramatically diminished in the U.S. as private/family debt has risen. Nowadays, our savings rate has diminished to 3.8%, according to a recent study (June 2017) by the Bureau of Economic Analysis.

Thus, our income in the 1950s had dramatically increased from the 1930s and '40s, but so has our debt, ever since the 1950s.

2. Fair Taxation

1953

Married Filing Jointly			Married Filing Separately			Single		
Marginal Tax Rate	Tax Brackets Over	But Not Over	Marginal Tax Rate	Tax Brackets Over	But Not Over	Marginal Tax Rate	Tax Brackets Over	But Not Over
			22.2%	$0	$2,000			
Applicable marginal tax rates are determined by the bracket (Married Filing Separately) corresponding to one-half of taxable income.			24.6%	$2,000	$4,000	Same as Married Filing Separately		
			29.0%	$4,000	$6,000			
			34.0%	$6,000	$8,000			
			38.0%	$8,000	$10,000			
			42.0%	$10,000	$12,000			
			48.0%	$12,000	$14,000			
			53.0%	$14,000	$16,000			
			56.0%	$16,000	$18,000			
			59.0%	$18,000	$20,000			
			62.0%	$20,000	$22,000			
			66.0%	$22,000	$26,000			
			67.0%	$26,000	$32,000			
			68.0%	$32,000	$38,000			
			72.0%	$38,000	$44,000			
			75.0%	$44,000	$50,000			
			77.0%	$50,000	$60,000			
			80.0%	$60,000	$70,000			
			83.0%	$70,000	$80,000			
			85.0%	$80,000	$90,000			
			88.0%	$90,000	$100,000			
			90.0%	$100,000	$150,000			
			91.0%	$150,000	$200,000			
			92.0%	$200,000				

Note: Tax rates include normal tax of 3 percent plus applicable surtax, and the maximum effective tax rate on net income was 88 percent. Last k

In 1944-45, when people actually paid for their wars, our income tax rate was 94%. It was never higher, before or afterwards.

---

[48] *The Average American Saves Less Than 5%, so How Are You Doing?* (<u>Los Angeles Times</u> reprint of article from Nerdwallet, August 19, 2017)

In June 2001, President Bush signed a bill making enormous tax cuts part of our political landscape. They were set to expire in 2012. However, with the advent of 9/11, plus the wars in Afghanistan and Iraq, as well as the buildup of a huge new component to the military-industrial complex, i.e., the intelligence services on steroids, government spending was completely out of control. A bi-partisan "supercommittee" was unable to tackle the then-$15 trillion federal budget deficit. Simon Johnson, professor of entrepreneurship at MIT's Sloan School of Management and former chief economist of the International Monetary Fund (IMF), called the tax cuts "inappropriate, excessive and irresponsible."[49]

During the 2016 Presidential campaign, and for several years before that, Congressional Republicans called for passage of additional tax cuts. Trump made that his clarion call, even though his base was largely exempt from any of the so-called benefits of the proposed cuts. Nonetheless, the Sheldon Adelsons, the DeVos family, the Mercers, the Koch Brothers, and other centa-millionaires and billionaires all thought it completely right that they (the top 1/100th of the 1%) should be able to obtain even more tax relief, for themselves and for their corporations.

Right wing think-tanks and thought leaders made much ado about this, with the result that in December 2017 Congress passed new tax legislation that will permanently keep corporate rates reduced from their 35% rate to 21%; over the next decade provide only marginal relief for ordinary taxpayers (everyone other than the top 1%), which relief will go away in 2027; and which will cause our federal deficit to increase by another $1.5 trillion.

The Congressional Republicans have short memories (or selective amnesia), since many of them were in office when the mid-2001 cuts were made, and certainly many of them remember the *sturm und drang* during the time of the Supercommittee's existence, when many more liberal members of Congress and outside observers thought it vitally important to restore taxes to more reasonable levels. There was

---

[49] **Dominc Rushe**, *The Bush-era Tax Cuts That Sank the Supercommittee* (<u>The Manchester Guardian</u>, November 21, 2011)

much objective evidence to confirm that the tax cuts had a massive, negative effect on the American economy.

Indeed, in a major report by the non-partisan Center on Budget and Policy Priorities (*Economic Downturn and Bush Policies Continue to Drive Large Projected Deficits*), May 10, 2011) it was determined that government spending under President Barack Obama was not the prime reason for today's massive deficit. "The fact remains, the economic downturn, President Bush's tax cuts and the wars in Afghanistan and Iraq explain virtually the entire deficit over the next ten years," the center concluded.

Instead of aggressively tackling the huge (over $20 trillion) national deficit, Republicans recently passed the law which makes it far worse. Apparently, they did not learn the lessons from the Center's report, which concluded that "the Bush-era tax cuts did not spur economic growth and had made a significant contribution to the deficit. Scrapping the tax cuts for the wealthy alone would be enough to make up for the shortfall in social security; scrapping them entirely would halt the rise in the national debt over the next decade."

Behind the rants of the rich was an ideology holding that low taxes will help the economy, while high taxes will destroy it. Considering we hit the Great Recession with a top rate of thirty-five percent, we must have been paying virtually nothing in taxes during the record 1950s boom years. Perhaps 10%? Maybe lower?

Try 91%.

Business Insider's Henry Blodget analyzed tax rates since 1912 and found periods of high taxation corresponded to strong growth, while low taxation *always* heralded a ***massive crash***. In his report, dated July 12, 2011, Blodget concluded as follows:

- **Today's government spending levels are indeed too high, at least relative to the average level of tax revenue the government has generated over the past 60 years.** Unless Americans were willing to radically increase the amount of taxes they pay relative to GDP, government spending must be cut.

- **Today's income taxes are strikingly low relative to the rates of the past century, especially for rich people.** (In fact, they have never been lower.) For most of the last century, including some boom times, top-bracket income tax rates were much higher than they are today.

- **Contrary to what Republicans would have you believe, super-high tax rates on rich people do not appear to hurt the economy or make people lazy:** During 1954 - 1964, the top bracket income tax rate was 91%--and the economy, middle-class, and stock market boomed.
- **Super-law tax rates on rich people also appear to be correlated with unsustainable 'sugar highs' in the economy**---brief, enjoyable booms followed by protracted busts. They also appear to be correlated with very high wage and other forms of inequality) For example, see the 1920s and now).
- **Periods of very low tax rates have been followed by periods with very high tax rates**

In the 1950s, the government raised taxes and people paid them.

And taxes stayed pretty much just that way for the next 15 years, until the early 1960s. Importantly, this was one of the most successful eras in U.S. economic history. The middle class boomed, the economy boomed, and the stock market boomed. And all with the top marginal income tax rate over 90%. This suggests that the Republican <u>mantra</u> about high marginal tax rates killing the economy is, well, a bunch of crap.

As a general matter of fairness and common sense, commodities of which are both in short supply these days, our parents and grandparents did not think that it was appropriate for multimillionaires and billionaires to pay less in taxes than their cleaning lady.

Today, we have apotheosized the wealthy and wish them "nothing but success." That charitable benediction belies the less-charitable prelude to Mario Puzo's *The Godfather*:

Behind every great fortune lies a crime. --- Honoré de Balzac

---

It is not the acquisition of wealth *per se* which is the problem. Instead, it is the refusal to relinquish any portion of it which has fueled the tax debate. It is their sense of entitlement to great wealth as a "natural right" which reminds one of the imperious attitudes of the old British aristocracy during England's days of Empire.

Now, making more money than ever, and with income-gaps at all-time highs, the wealthy want more of the pie and want to keep more of it. *This* is the "entitlement mentality" about which people should be complaining. And it is this mentality, and the legislative action by Republicans supporting it, that will give rise to the next crash. It is unknown exactly when the crash will take place, but it is expected sometime in the next couple of years, and it **will** be ugly.

In the immortal words of Samuel L. Jackson in *Jurassic Park*, "hold onto your butts."

3. Less Crime

Despite what the media tells us, crime is falling.[50] You're less likely to be murdered now than at any time in the last twenty years, though not as safe as you would have been in 1957. That's when the murder rate bottomed out at four people per 100,000, the lowest in fifty five years. Before that it spent three years hovering around 4.1, which is still pretty good. To compare, from 1969 and 1997, it remained over seven. (<u>Crime in the United States, FBI, Uniform Crime Reports.</u>) So all those stories your grandma told about being able to leave her door unlocked at night and letting her kids play alone in abandoned warehouses are completely true.

In short, there was no need for "helicopter parents" or, if they had had them, cell phones given to three- and four-year olds. It was normal for children to walk or bicycle to and from school; to play all day long on the weekend; to experience different levels of freedom, based on age and circumstances.

---

[50] "U.S. Crime Figures: Why the Drop?," (BBC News, June 21, 2011)

Much of this "free-range parenting," which avoided overparenting and overprotection, was based on two factors: the 1946 release of the best-selling book by "America's pediatrician," Dr. Benjamin Spock[51], and the *Zeitgeist* of suburban America. The communities were safe; everybody was about the same age, had the same types of homes, worked in the same types of jobs, and relaxed after the Second World War and the Korean War. In short, a highly-respected pediatrician said that it was "OK" to give children a reasonable amount of personal freedom and its corresponding responsibility, and the spirit of the day said that times were good and communities were havens for our families.

This sense was mirrored in the TV shows we watched: "wholesome, family shows," such as "The Mickey Mouse Club," "Davy Crockett," "Walt Disney Presents," "Leave It to Beaver," "Captain Kangaroo," "Lunch With Soupy Sales," "Howdy Doody," "Father Knows Best," "Adventures of Ozzie & Harriet," "Dragnet," "Make Room for Daddy," "Gunsmoke," "Have Gun Will Travel," "The Lone Ranger," "I Love Lucy," "Lassie," "The Honeymooners," and many others.

The themes were patriarchal and family-centric, for the most part, although there were a few Westerns ("Gunsmoke," "Have Gun Will Travel," "The Lone Ranger") which televised cowboys-versus-Indians or "White Hats versus Black Hats" stories with six-shooters drawn.

(Contrast this with the social unrest during the 1960s: the Civil Rights, anti-war, and women's rights movements, plus the hippies' counter-culture lifestyles, and our society no longer felt safe and secure.)

People in the Generation X demographic (those born between 1965 and 1984) were raised in an era of turmoil and chaos. Instead of having a well-plotted life course in front of them, they faced increasing urbanization, with so-called "race riots" throughout many cities.

---

[51] **Spock, M.D., Benjamin,** *The Common Sense Book of Baby and Child Care* (Duell, Sloan and Pearce, 1946)

The young people born in the late 1940s and early 1950s were now facing being drafted to fight in the War in Vietnam. Many of them joined the anti-war movement because they viewed our involvement in Vietnam as part of a dying, imperialistic legacy which had no place in modern America. Secretary of Defense Robert McNamara, the former head of Ford Motor Company, created and implemented "policy analysis" as part of American military (and later political) culture, and the young people who were being treated as cannon fodder deeply resented the mechanistic way they were fed into the military and returned home in body bags.

In 1963, when *The Feminine Mystique* was published, its author, Betty Friedan, really launched the second phase of the feminist movement.

Women were freed from automatically becoming mothers when they had sex, courtesy of the recent invention of the birth-control pill. But it was not only reproductive freedom that women sought: they also fought for choice, for personal autonomy in how their bodies and minds and souls would be used and expressed, and they were not content to be treated as mindless chattels, as second-class citizens.

In the face of the feminist movement, many men were left in the dark. Some separatist and revolutionary feminists were not interested in interaction with men, and many other feminist groups found working in mixed-sex groups to be unproductive. The backlash to all this was that many marriages dissolved, with kids the victims.

Thus, children born into the "social cauldron" of the 1960s through the 1980s found themselves the products of single-parent homes, with great personal and social uncertainty all around them, confronted with drug and/or alcohol abuse, and a kind of "collective neurosis" permeating our country. Perhaps "social schizophrenia" might be a more apt term.

Consider the "Silent Majority" of the late 1960s. Imagine them facing people with heavy drug usage, counter-culture attitudes, and a much more progressive lifestyle. In the 1980s, AIDS came to the forefront of our national consciousness. Additionally, they also saw a huge increase in cocaine usage, the "War on Drugs," the "Hare

Krishna" and other Asian religious groups, a kind of "hippies-on-steroids" culture.

In the latter part of the 1980s, the "McMartin Scandal" was nationwide news, in which the networks were constantly broadcasting the day-care sex-abuse hysteria. The trial lasted from 1987 to 1990, but all charges were dropped, and there were no convictions.

Nonetheless, in the aftermath of the McMartin case, parents throughout the country became overprotective and started their "helicopter parenting" strategies, shielding their children from any kind of free time away from the parents. As Lenore Skenazy writes in her book,[52] it hurts the personal development of children when they are completely shielded from, and do not learn how to deal with, real-world risk. Mom and Dad won't be here forever, and it is vital that the kids learn how to cope with and manage risk as a healthy part of growing up.

The *dénouement* of the McMartin case was that a large part of the country was brainwashed into thinking that their precious little children were about to be snatched up, molested, or even worse by perverts and child-abusers lurking around every corner.

These Gen X parents were so often scared of their own shadows that they completely missed the point of raising children: you have to teach them independence by granting them appropriate levels of freedom and responsibility. Hovering over them throughout childhood, adolescence, and even into adulthood has many insidious effects: neurosis, over-dependence, and lack of self-reliance, not attractive qualities nor suitable ones for mature adults.

4. Access to Education

Get an education, earn more. It's that simple.

From 1944 through 1956, the G.I. Bill gave returning service personnel an opportunity to get technical or liberal arts education, on

---

[52] **Skenazy, Lenore,** *Free Range Kids: Giving Our Children the Freedom We Had Without Going Nuts with Worry* (John Wiley & Sons, 2009)

Uncle Sam's dime. These former soldiers, sailors, marines, and airmen, would almost certainly not been able to afford college without the government picking up the tab. The G.I. Bill was later extended, and although it doesn't pay for everything, it was quite a godsend for the 7.8 million veterans of World War II, and the 2.4 million veterans of the Korean War.[53]

The post-Korean War economy was becoming rapidly modernized. Manufacturers were deeply in need of people who could design, build, and operate manufacturing lines; tools, dies, and other equipment; who could become engineers, machinists, draftsmen; and who understood the intricacies of complex manufacturing processes. Education was essential for these purposes, and as students graduated, they were able to quickly get jobs that would allow them to buy houses, cars, save money, and raise families.

In short, the G.I. Bill built the American Middle Class.

That was then, this is now. In the 2000s, education is ridiculously expensive for quality schools, and with the shortage of manufacturing jobs in the United States, the only substantive forms of employment are dead-end, low-pay service jobs or high-cost, high-end knowledge jobs. The main problem is that our manufacturing base has been largely off-shored. The manufacture of goods, commodities, retail items, all provided a solid path to the middle class. Non-Ivy League students could get a good crafts education in high school, maybe a little in a technical course in a community college or vocational school, and they would be able to support themselves and their families as part of the middle class. They could afford housing, cars, vacations, savings, and they had decent life styles. Nowadays, it takes two and three incomes to do, poorly, what one income could accomplish with grace.

In the 1950s, education really saved this country. It allowed manufacturing to be the top dog in our economy. Today, manufacturing is such a small part that it has become consigned to "arts-and-crafts" status.

---

[53] Stephen Barr, *Long After WWII, The GI Bill Lives On* (Washington Post, Sunday, May 30, 2004)

Ariana Huffington aptly described the death of manufacturing and the rise of our financial industry: "In America, we used to make things; now, we just make things up!"

It's fascinating---and tragic---to compare the costs of education two generations ago (graduating in 1970) and now.

In 1970, a year of tuition at a public university cost $1,207. I attended California State University, Los Angeles, starting in 1970. I paid for my own schooling with part-time work. By contrast, in the most recent year of data available, a moderate college budget for an in-state public college for the 2017–2018 academic year averaged $25,290. A moderate budget at a private college averaged $50,900. That's a 2095.3% increase in the cost of a four year degree.

(http://www.collegedata.com/cs/content/content_payarticle_tmpl. html?articled=10064)

It's even more appalling to compare the costs of education in 2015 and their projected costs in 2033.

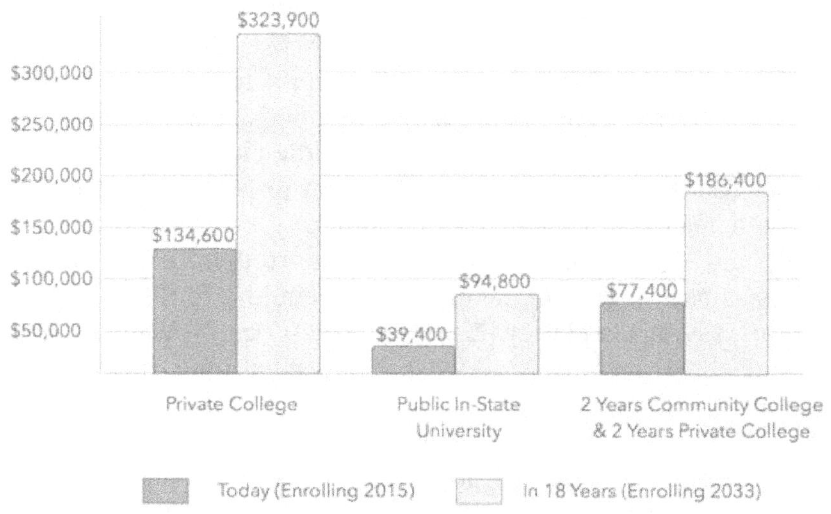

A chart from SavingForCollege.com, based on data from The College Board, reflects multiple college options in 2015 and 2033.

Suppose you're earning minimum wage and trying to make it through college.

In 1970, you could work 755 hours at a minimum wage job over the course of a year to earn enough to pay for a year of schooling at a public institution – about 14 hours per week. That was almost exactly what my work schedule was like when I paid for my own schooling.

In 2010, you would have to work 1,823 hours at a minimum wage job over the course of a year to earn enough money to pay for a year of schooling at a public institution – about 35 hours per week.

In 2019, you had to work more than a 40 hour week to barely get by.

In other words, in 1970, you could work a part time job as a cashier or something to that effect and easily pay for college, enabling you to work and attend college without going into debt. In 2019, you'd have to work a full time-plus job to pay for college, meaning you essentially have to choose between debt and an education or some other difficult plan.

Not only that, a college education is becoming much more of a requirement than it was in 1970. In 1973, about 72% of the jobs available for U.S. workers required a high school diploma or less. In 2018, that number dropped to 38%, and future projections show it only going lower. The jobs remaining that do not require a college education are primarily service jobs that do not pay a high wage. The chart below reflects this trend.

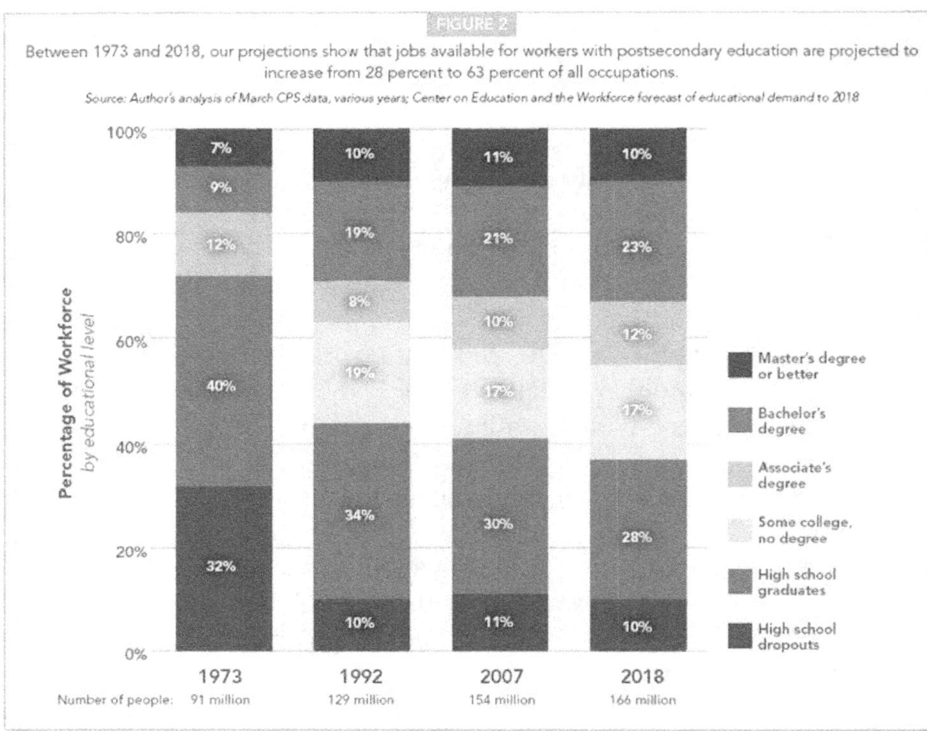

In other words, in 1970, the choice to enter the workforce immediately after high school or work a minimum wage job while going to college was a real choice. Today, it's not a real choice unless you want to agree to low income for life. You have to enter the costly bargain of secondary education.

If you can't work more than 40 hours a week and attend school, then college loans may be available, but at what price? You will pay interest; you may pay late fees and other costs; and you will not be able to file for bankruptcy protection to avoid your college loan obligations.

You may be able to get some leverage over you loan(s) should you go into public-sector or nonprofit organization work. Should you become a nurse, or a teacher, or a police officer or a fire-fighter, then if you work in that capacity for 10 years, you can avoid paying back your student debt. This is sometimes trickier than it may seem, since a lot of the companies handling student loans often mishandle the collection aspects and erroneously list people as delinquent when, due to minor clerical errors, they missed some paperwork or didn't file it in the right location at the right time, or the student loan companies mistakenly reported on the loans.[54]

But suppose you've completed your education; then what?

To paraphrase The Narrator in *Fight Club*, we're "slaves with white collars," working in jobs we hate, with people we don't like, so we can buy crap we don't need, to impress people who could care less.

Such is our society now, compared to the 1950s. We don't make many things here in America. These days, we mostly shuffle paper, use fancy words to try to describe what it is we are supposedly doing, to earn income which may, with the advent of artificial intelligence, no longer be ours to claim within the next 10 years.

Education is more desperately needed than ever, but for a new world with new industries and businesses we can barely imagine.

5. Spending Power

Between WWII and 1970, purchasing power exploded. In those more patriarchal times, a husband working a blue collar job could provide for his entire family. According to Nobel Prize winning economist Paul Krugman, this was largely thanks to a third of America's workforce being unionized, meaning any manager who mistreated his workers was about to open up a can of whup-ass.[55]

Money went further too: minimum wage earners could cover their rent with slightly over a week's full-time work, meaning even those at the bottom had money to spare. In fact, the only people who saw their lifestyles slip in this period were top executives—who saw their incomes drop into line with everyone else's.[56]

---

[54] Andrew Josuweit, *5 Common Student Loan Credit Reporting Errors -- and How to Fix Them* (<u>Forbes</u>, October 15, 2017)

[55] Paul Krugman, *The Twinkie Manifesto* (the <u>New York Times</u>, November 18, 2012)

[56] *Id.*

Here are some interesting point-of-sale pricing comparisons between the 1950s and now. I looked at minimum wage; how much a gallon of gas cost; how much a movie ticket cost; and the average cost of rent. Notice that up until Reaganomics took over, minimum wage was almost a living wage; with the advent of "Supply-Side" or "trickle-down" economics in Ronald Reagan's first term as President, the path towards a decent standard of living was no longer possible for someone earning minimum wage.

1950s
Minimum wage: $0.75/hour
Gas: $0.27 or 22 minutes of work
Movie ticket: $0.48 or 38 minutes of work
Rent: $42 or 56 hours of work

1960s
Minimum wage: $1/hour
Gas: $0.31 or 19 minutes of work
Movie ticket: $0.69 or 41 minutes of work
Rent: $71 or 71 hours of work

1970s
Minimum wage: $1.60/hour
Gas: $0.36 or 14 minutes of work
Movie ticket: $1.55 or 58 minutes of work
Rent: $108 or 67.5 hours of work

1980s
Minimum wage: $3.10/hour
Gas: $1.25 or 24 minutes of work
Movie ticket: $2.60 or 50 minutes of work
Rent: $243 or 78 hours of work

Fast forward to today and the minimum wage buys nothing, while inequality is the worst it's been since the Great Depression. In this *Billions* environment, the plutocrats, their armies of servants, multiple mansions, and yachts are all back, and any hint of sharing the income with anyone other than the top 1/100th of the top 1% was given the heretical brand "socialist."

6. The Suburbs

Today we think of the suburbs as a hotbed of depression, anxiety, and sex with your girlfriend's mother (sorry, Mrs. Robinson). But in the 1950s they were meant to symbolize everything that was great about modern America. And they did.

For a huge chunk of the American public, the suburbs represented their first chance to get out of the inner city and into their own house. Before World War II, the younger generation mostly rented dingy apartments and concentrated on saving up for a bigger place, typically a two- or three-bedroom flat.

To the children of the 1940s, the suburbs were a huge step up. Suddenly you had light, space, a bit of land and a place to call your own. Best of all, they gave the growing middle class something to aim for—a reason to work hard and keep the economy growing. So much of America's economy depended on suburban developments and the pride of ownership they gave to their occupants.

In 1947, a building entrepreneur, Abraham Levitt, and his two sons, William and Alfred, broke ground on a planned community on former farmland in Nassau County, Long Island, New York. By the early 1950s, this community---Levittown---was home to over 17,000 families. In those days of racially restrictive covenants, before the Supreme Court case of ***Shelley v. Kraemer***[57] prohibited racial restrictions on the purchase and sale of real property, the Levittown homes were only available to World War II veterans and their families, and only *white* veterans at that. The cost of these homes was $6,990, with almost no money down.

Not long after the Long Island development, new Levittown communities were built in New Jersey and Pennsylvania. Throughout the 1950s, millions of tract homes were constructed. Schools,

---

[57] *Shelley v. Kraemer* (1948) 334 U.S. 1

hospitals, churches, shopping centers, were all erected, month after month, year after year.

After years of growth in these planned communities, it became clear that "white flight" was an entrenched feature of the modern housing market throughout the country.[58]

For whites, life in suburbia was much better than life in crowded, deteriorated urban settings. For non-whites, suffering from the effects of segregated housing, life was not so good.

What continued the pattern of segregated housing were several behaviors: racist builders and realtors refused to sell to non-white buyers; mortgage lenders practiced mortgage discrimination; redlining; and insurance discrimination also contributed. It took many lawsuits, protests, and pressure on legislators before the most egregious aspects of housing discrimination were eliminated.

---

[58] Bogue, Donald J. and Emerson Seim, *Components of Population Change in Suburban and Central City Populations of Standard metropolitan Areas: 1940 to 1950* (<u>Rural Sociology,</u> Sept-Dec 1956)

7. Social Mobility

The basic idea of the American Dream is that anyone who works hard will be rewarded. You start off poor, you keep yourself open to opportunities, you work hard, and thirty years later you are able to retire with great wealth, having risen far above wherever you started. Economic class was not a factor in your life plans. The fifties took that dream and ran with it: a child born in the USA post-WWII was more than twice as likely to graduate as one born literally anywhere else in the Western world.[59] This trend continued right through to the early seventies, at which point neoliberalism reared its head.

Skip forward to now and we've gone from being the best to the worst. We are a class-based society, where your father's income is largely determinative of what your income will be. Studies from the London School of Economics and the University of Ottawa revealed that economic class is now a fundamental problem with our social mobility.[60] According to economist Robert Reich, forty-two percent of children now born into poverty will stay there, a higher percentage than in countries that still have kings. In 2018 the American Dream has nothing to do with hard work—and everything to do with who your parents are.

8. Optimism

In television and movies, setting something in the 1950s sent a shorthand message for things like "nostalgia" and "optimism." When you look at everything else on this list, it makes sense--but how, exactly, do you measure optimism?

Beginning in 1935, Polling Company AIPO spent decades calling strangers and asking them how happy they were—a move that actually yielded usable data. According to *Economics and Happiness:*

---

[59] **Sean Coughlan**, *Downward Mobility Haunts U.S. Education* (<u>BBC News</u>, December 3, 2012)

[60] **Jerome Karabel**, *Grand Illusion: Mobility, Inequality, and the American Dream* (<u>Huffington Post</u>, October 2, 2012)

Framing the Analysis[61], the 1950s saw a surge of people claiming they were very happy, peaking between 1955 and 1960 at around forty percent. That's the highest it's ever been. Remember this isn't just "happy" but "very happy"—as in nothing could possibly be better. A different study measuring average happiness across the decades also placed the 1950s as peak smiling time, with everything going downhill after that, right up until our groaning present.[62]

9. Falling Debt

As discussed above, we had high debt right after World War II. However, with high taxes and an expanding economy, per capita debt had gone down and as a society it had been cut dramatically because of our country's fiscal discipline.

Now, without the excuse of a global war, our debt is back at its World War II peak, and it is likely to continue escalating rapidly, as the result of the recent tax cuts.

10. National Popularity

After World War II, American military might was unsurpassed. The Soviet Union, having lost some 27 million people, and having had so much of its infrastructure destroyed, was not an immediate threat. Our former enemies in Germany, Italy, Spain and Japan, presided over moribund militaries and economies. However, in the spirit of generosity (and more than a little enlightened self-interest), we extended the hand of financial help through the Marshall Plan, and the redevelopment programs implemented by General Douglas MacArthur. We did not want the resurgence of angry military forces after World War II that we saw after the first World War.

---

[61] *Economics and Happiness: Framing the Analysis*, eds. L. Bruni, P.L. Porta (<u>Oxford University Press</u>, 2005)

[62] *International Differences in Well-Being*, eds. Ed Diener, John F. Helliwell, and Daniel Kahneman (<u>Oxford University Press</u>, 2010)

There was a spirit of freedom throughout the world. Great Britain's colonial empire was dissolving; likewise, for other European powers in Africa and Asia. The United States seemed to be the sole world power based on stability and justice (at least, that was the ruse we used to convince countries to repose their trust in us in the post-War world). We spoke of freedom, and we opposed the expansionist programs of the communists.

During the 1950s, while we were ramping up our military-industrial complex, we were also providing substantial economic and other assistance through relatively generous contributions of foreign aid through our Agency for International Development (AID). The agency provided technology transfer, farming assistance, and political support.

During the 1950s, we were paranoid about the so-called communist threat, and engaged in years of saber-rattling against the Soviets and their allies. (Of course, few Americans were aware of our own belligerent conduct towards the Soviets, including surrounding them with missiles; radio broadcasting to them and their neighbors, with the Voice of America's and Radio Free Europe's propaganda; engaging in constant espionage and attempts to sabotage the Soviets' military; and so on.)

Regardless of the unyielding hostility we displayed towards our former ally, the Soviet Union, we presented a friendly face to most of the rest of the world. With our Hollywood entertainment industry extolling our virtues, the U.S. was able to couch much of what we did in terms that would appeal to most countries: we were victors, but we were generous; we had great strength, but we weren't cruel; we sought peace and justice for all who believed in democracy.

Contrast that to our involvement in the Vietnam War; our support of dictatorships in Africa, the Middle East, Asia, and Latin America; our foreign policy miscues that made it clear that we were not as purely motivated as previously broadcast. Imagine, further, the reaction of the world when it learned of our xenophobia, racism, and cultural bigotry. Their favorable responses from the 1950s began to wane.

Add to that our wars in Afghanistan and Iraq, the lies we told and the blunders we made in order to justify sending troops there, and it is easy to understand why, at this date, there is hostility towards us.

The proverbial frosting on the cake, of course, was the election of Donald J. Trump to be our 45th President. From his mouth, and the mouths of his current and former Cabinet members and advisers, they learned of America's extraordinary bigotry and religious intolerance, racism, and bias against non-Americans, and the great residue of love and appreciation for us evaporated like the morning dew in the sun.

The conclusion to this discussion of the differences between the 1950s America and the America of 2019 shows that in many respects our social difficulties stem from a fundamental problem, lack of tax revenues. The parsimonious attitude towards providing the government with sufficient revenue to fund education, health, infrastructure, science and technology, foreign aid programs, and many other aspects of life we enjoyed in the 1950s came to us courtesy of Ronald Reagan's presidency and the Reaganomics the president espoused. As demonstrated elsewhere, "trickle down" economics was not the approach for a living wage in America, nor was it a strategy designed to help us keep the friendships we previously enjoyed around the world.

In this country, we paid taxes and got substantial services in return. The trade-off between taxes paid and services received contributed to a strong society. With the advent of neoliberalism in the 1970s and afterwards came the Faustian bargain with the "economic Devil" to whom we sold our societal soul, wherein we expressly chose not to be our brother's keeper in exchange for lower tax rates. (We ignored the wisdom of the old maxim: "We'd better take care of the poor---or, someday, the poor are going to 'take care' of us!")

And that, dear readers, is the legacy of "Uncle 'Dutch," the "Great Communicator," otherwise known as Ronald Reagan.

CHAPTER 16
GOOD JOBS AND FAIR TRADE

From 1793 to 1981, America had substantial tariffs imposed on foreign-made finished goods. We chose not to impose tariffs on raw materials not available here in the United States, since our goal was to get the cheapest raw materials and transform them into finished goods, which we could then sell domestically and also export.

Since the advent of neoliberalism when Ronald Reagan took office in 1981, we reversed that plan. Now, instead of being the largest importer of raw materials and the largest exporter of finished goods, we now export gasoline and natural gas; coal; lumber; and many other resources which are parts of our national patrimony. Prior to Ronald Reagan's presidency, the United States was the biggest creditor nation and made the greatest number of exports of high-quality finished goods. This was when we still had a substantial manufacturing base and focused on production of appliances, capital equipment, and consumer merchandise. But by 1985, the U.S. shifted its position and became the world's largest debtor nation.[63]

Previously, China shipped out cheap goods and lots of raw materials. Now, China exports plenty of finished goods to the U.S., and it will soon be the world's largest economy. Why did we shift 180 degrees of our long-established practices regarding tariffs?

Neoliberalism was a concept of the 20th-century resurgence of 19th-century ideas associated with *laissez-faire* economic liberalism.

---

[63] Peter T. Kilborn, *U.S. Turns Into Debtor Nation* (<u>New York Times</u>, September 17, 1985)

It was the economic aspect of the conservatism of Ronald Reagan and his political colleagues who came up with "supply-side" or "trickle-down" economics, who predicated their beliefs on the notion that individual decision-making should have paramount importance, and that government forces should be as restricted as possible. This theory said that "the market" should make pricing decisions and government should get out of the way.

The problem with this theory is that it creates the conditions leading to a "race to the bottom." The manufacturing process did well in this country from its inception, which coincided with the Industrial Revolution. Our policies were based on the theories and writings of America's first Secretary of the Treasury, Alexander Hamilton, who strongly advocated a robust tariff system as the number one means of assuring the creation and maintenance of good American jobs.

Hamilton's basic thesis was simple and straightforward. Government should create incentives through tariffs, import and export quotas, and subsidies ("bounties") to help industrial development in newly-competitive markets and/or industries. His view could be summarized thusly: let us import wood, which we can then engineer and manufacture to make an axe handle out of it. The handle would be attached to an axe, which would then be used to fell timber, which would be used to build a house, and create many jobs with it. The creation of value was the essential *sine qua non* of our nation's economic health.

Hamilton articulated his views in *Alexander Hamilton's Report on the Subject of Manufactures*, December 5, 1791. His 11 points regarding tariffs, quotas, duties, and drawbacks expressed a fundamentally wise understanding of why value creation was the backbone of a country's economy, and why a proper understanding of the role foreign trade could play was essential in building that economy.

For much of America's history, we largely followed Hamilton's guidance. Even up to the eve of World War II, Customs duties (tariffs) were the largest single item of income for the federal government.

In the decades after World War II, the American economy was still focused on manufacturing. Along with our manufacturing capabilities was the concomitant of unionism. At our economic peak, in the 1950s, about 35% of America's work force was unionized. Local, state, and federal elections felt the effect of union efforts for many years. Laws to repeal child labor; achieve the 40-hour work week; establish workplace safety; attain the minimum wage, as well as overtime pay, were just a few of the contributions to American economic strength due to union activity.

Unions and capital had always been at odds. Ideologically, unions represented the collective interest, whereas capital had its "lone wolf" mentality. For years, there was an uneasy relationship between the forces of money and the power of labor, and they more or less existed in a kind of tense working balance from about the mid-19th to the mid-20th centuries.

Capital considered labor to be composed of inferior people, lacking education or the other *accoutrements* of "class." However, labor was a "necessary evil" if manufacturing was to succeed. Conversely, labor viewed the monied class as being composed of avaricious, money-grubbers who had little understanding of how things were built/manufactured, little understanding of human nature, little understanding of anything other than the acquisition of money.

Due to the struggles of labor to obtain better treatment in American factories, there were often strikes, work slow-downs, boycotts, and other forms of concerted labor action. Employers, especially in the late 1800s up through the 1930s, resorted to brute force and, many times, employed armed gangs of thugs to break up strikes, intimidate union members, kidnap or kill union leaders, and otherwise thwart the efforts of unions to achieve economic justice.

The culmination of the bitter capital-labor conflict was the Ludlow Massacre of April 20, 1914, when the Colorado National Guard was called in to attack a tent colony of 1,200 striking coal miners in Ludlow, Colorado. The National Guard used machine guns to fire into the compound, killing dozens of strikers, as well as their wives and children.[64]

---

[64] Howard Zinn, *A People's History of the United States: 1492-Present*, pp. 346-349 (Harper & Row, 1980)

Because of the violence between the owners and workers, the courts had to come into the picture and mediate a kind of truce between the two forces. Especially during the terrible times of the Great Depression in the 1930s, the America labor movement felt that it was compelled to associate with socialist and even communist organizations in order to muster a more effective counterbalance to the power of the business owners. For approximately 25 years the labor movement was subjected to the anti-labor blatherings of the popular press and had to fight popular sentiment against the socialists and the communists, especially right after World War II.

Government forces, e.g., the National Labor Relations Board; the EEOC; the courts, all had to interpose counterweights to the powerful interests of capital. Without government intervention in the 1950s through the '70s, labor would have been in a completely moribund state. Thus, government forces saved unions from capital's destructive power.

However, when the conservatives (neoliberals) came to power in Reagan's administration they felt that government "should be small enough to drown in a bathtub." That included limited roles of tariffs, import quotas, and other means of restricting unfair trade practices of foreign countries. And of course it meant doing away with unions. In fact, President Reagan's first act as President was to disband P.A.T.C.O., the air traffic controllers union, when they went on strike in August 1981. After that, it was open season on all working-class unions.

Today, only about 10.5 percent of America's workforce is now unionized.[65]

This is my opinion, only, but it seems to me that the neoliberal attitude implanted into the psyches of Republicans, starting in 1980, was really the beginning of a more insidious---and final---way to break the back of unions and eliminate collective bargaining power. Right-to-work states, those which prohibit unions from requiring that workers join or pay union dues, now amount to 28 of the 50 states.

---

[65] News Release, United States Dept. of Labor, Bureau of Labor Statistics (Washington, D.C., Jan. 18, 2019)

(http://www.ncsl.org/research/labor-and-employment/right-to-work-laws-and-bills.aspx).

Perhaps it's as simple as this. Reagan and the toadies in his Cabinet wanted to please their corporate overlords by putting the final nail in the American labor movement's coffin. So long as unions existed there was always the danger that collective action might overcome the nefarious actions of the business owners. Lawsuits, labor action, education programs, all might be called upon to help level the playing field between labor and capital. Capital wanted none of that. How to address that problem? Simple:

ELIMINATE AMERICA'S MANUFACTURING BASE.

The ideological fervor of the increasingly rightist Republican leadership against labor and in favor of capital became so strong during the 1970s and 1980s that it can be argued that these ideologues literally gave up on the American economy in order to create the conditions of burying labor.

When Jack E. Welch, the CEO of General Electric, mandated offshoring and outsourcing so that American manufacturing businesses would cut their labor forces in America by more than 50% by the beginning of 1990, and when virtually all manufacturing was conducted overseas, that was bad. But when white-collar jobs for lawyers, accountants, engineers, designers, began to relocate to Bangalore, Manila, Romania, and other locales where labor was cheap, that was the end of job stability in the United States. And it was at that point that we built our own fiscal coffin and managed to ensconce ourselves therein.

The idea of outsourcing and offshoring American jobs was based on Jack Welch's mantra that "public corporations owed their allegiance to stockholders, not employees." Therefore, Welch said, "companies should seek to lower costs and maximize profits by moving operations wherever it's cheapest." Welch, who was widely respected by other corporate chieftains, came up with the talismanic phrase which justified the evisceration of the American Middle Class and the manufacturing base on which it was founded.[66]

Without a trace of irony, Bill Clinton - who campaigned as a progressive, but governed as a right-winger, economically speaking - pushed ahead with NAFTA, CAFTA, and other terrible programs that increased our offshoring of jobs.

WHAT IS THE SOLUTION?

The countries that have demonstrated the greatest economic growth over the last 50 - 60 years are the ones who actually practiced the principles articulated by Secretary Hamilton almost 230 years ago. Korea, Japan, and China, in particular, used tariffs, quotas, export restrictions, government subsidies, and related research and development programs to help develop new industries.

In Japan, for example, the Ministry of International Trade and Industry (MITI) provided huge support to industries such as automobiles, electronics, telecommunications, and consumer goods. With their help, Japanese cars went from being globally considered as junk to being the paradigms of high quality and luxury. Without MITI, there would be no Infinity, no Acura, and certainly no Lexus. Top-notch electronics, computers, telephones, and many other examples of consumer merchandise have led Japan to be one of the strongest economies in the world.

The same principle held true in South Korea. In the aftermath of World War II, and then the Korean War, South Korea was an economic ghost-town. It had virtually no industry, and what it made was of abysmal quality. But by converting from a dirt-poor, agrarian economy to one based on manufacturing, Korea has, over the past 60 years, gone from a fly-speck to the 12th largest economy in the world, just behind Russia.[67]

And now, China has ramped up its own capabilities in manufacturing. Have they stolen our technology, directly or through

---

[66] *Where America's Jobs Went* (*The Week*, March 18, 2011)

[67] **Ferdinand Bada,** *The World's 25 Biggest Economies* (World Atlas, March 1, 2018)

manipulation of foreign investment laws? Absolutely. Have they dramatically shifted their own tariffs, quotas, export restrictions, and subsidies programs? Obviously. And are they eating our economic lunch? Of course.

China is now basing its relentless push towards global technology dominance on major changes in its manufacturing (and tariff) structures. Formerly, a net exporter of raw materials and cheap labor, China has changed its laws to allow foreign investors to come into China---but with the *proviso* that technology must be transferred from the foreign owners to the Chinese. Additionally, the Chinese have a well-deserved reputation for stealing our technology. Moreover, the many thousands of Chinese students well-educated in America's post-graduate programs have acquired vast quantities of both theoretical and practical knowledge in terms of manufacturing and R & D practices, then have returned to China to share their knowledge and radically transform Chinese business practices.

Now, China is poised to become the world's leader in biotechnology; electronics; and pharmaceuticals.

Can the United States return the favor?

It will be painful for the ultra-wealthy to have to give up their positions of power, pealth, and privilege, but the short answer is "Yes!"

Here's an example. Suppose that a pair of Nike athletic shoes cost $1.00 to make in Indonesia but cost $15.00 to make in the U.S. The U.S. consumer would prefer to pay the lower price based on the Indonesian manufacturing cost. However, the consumer doesn't necessarily get that significantly lower cost, since Nike's duty (according to Jack Welch) is to its shareholders, not its employees (nor its consumers). So Nike charges an arm-and-a-leg for its athletic shoes sold in America.

If we returned to the Tariff Schedules of the United States that existed between 1954 and 1974, for example, we would be able to impose a tariff on those athletic shoes of $14.00 so that the total landed cost here in the U.S. was $15.00, the same price as the cost of domestic production.

That would tend to strongly reduce the desire to manufacture in the Third World and would lead to the restoration of American manufacturing jobs.

The same principle holds true with automobiles, clothing, appliances, electronics, and all manner of consumer goods.

"But, but....," sputter the neoliberals, "we are members of NAFTA, CAFTA, and the WTO. We have many multi-lateral treaties that we have to follow. What happens if we pull out? Won't that start a trade war?"

The popular media play that string constantly because it sells ad copy. The talking heads pontificate upon the implications of the U.S. withdrawing from the WTO and the other trade agreements and argue that doom and despair will follow if we do so.

Nonsense.

Yes, there will be periods of adjustment. Yes, there will be revisions to countries' tariffs and subsidies programs. Yes, some sectors will initially suffer, but others will dramatically return to the strengths they lost starting in the late 1970s and afterwards when the U.S. gave away the store.

Many analysts say that the restoration of tariffs and the related import laws would not necessarily reinstate our manufacturing base. This is because factories are increasingly replacing human workers with robots. The role of automation in displacing human workers may be exaggerated, however.

In a lengthy recent report,[68] the authors concluded that "The steep decline of U.S. manufacturing during the first decade of the century was the result of changes in trade policy not automation. During this period, manufacturing productivity growth actually slowed, averaging only 7 percent in all manufacturing sectors other than computer and electronics. **At the same time, the entrance of China into the World Trade Organization allowed the trade deficit to increase from $83 billion in 2001 to $347 billion and was responsible for 2.4 million**

---

[68] Stettner, Andrew; Yudken, Joel S.; and McCormack, Michael, *Why Manufacturing Jobs Are Worth Saving* (The Century Foundation, June 13, 2017)

job losses." (citing *The China Syndrome: Local Labor Market Effects of Important Competition in the United States*, David H. Autor, David Dorn, and Gordon H. Hanson, <u>American Economic Review</u>, Vol. 103, no. 6 (2013): 2121–168. [emphasis added]

President Trump started a trade war with China in 2019. China, not surprisingly, decided to reply with its own policies: tariffs and monetary manipulation, where they allowed the value of their currency, the *Renminbi*, to about 7 to 1 U.S. dollar. The sad reality is that Trump either does not understand tariffs or he has chosen to ignore how they work. His ham-fisted policies and practices are hurting U.S. consumers and also agriculture and manufacturers. However, once the tariff policies become clear, and tax policies are adjusted accordingly, it is likely that American farmers and manufacturers can once again return to pre-war profitability.

Despite temporary shortfalls, the net gain by a return to our old tariff regime, however, will be experienced in America's manufacturing base. Built on that base, America had a Middle Class that was strong. That Middle Class gave hope for social and economic mobility to people who were born in impoverished conditions. That Middle Class was the backbone of America.

We need to understand that not everyone is suited for a white-collar, high-cost/high-end job. Some people do better in the fields of manual labor and blue-collar work. There is nothing wrong with that, provided that these workers have good incomes with benefits that will allow them to support families and be productive members of society.

A return to the tariff policies we had for most of our history, along with the tax policies to support that return, would lead to a dramatic resurgence in American manufacturing. In short, it would lead to the restoration of the Middle Class and provide us with the strengths we formerly enjoyed for many years from the end of World War II to 1980.

CHAPTER 17
SEEDING THE GROUND

It is a commonplace among economists and owners/managers of small-to-medium sized enterprises (SMEs) that small businesses are, by far and away, the largest job creators in this country. About 70% of America's enterprises are Main Street businesses, with a significant number (two out of three) of new jobs created there.[69] Yet, it is also true that getting capital for startups is virtually impossible. Our capital formation structure for small business startups in the United States is broken.[70]

An enlightening article was authored by Stephan Aarsol, CEO and Founder of Tower Paddle Boards in San Diego, California.[71] In it, Mr. Aarsol advocated the use of federal funding, in the form of venture capital, to provide seed money for startups. His proposed structure would work like this:

- Federal government allocates $3 billion to fund 10,000 startups, or $300,000/company.
- Award investments "through a massively scaled, locally distributed business pitch competition, using the nation's top 200 universities to field entries"

---

[69] former SBA Administrator Karen G. Mills, *Who Are America's Job Creators?* (Washington Post, April 13, 2013)

[70] Ty Kissel, *Should the Federal Government Invest in Startups?* (Forbes, August 21, 2013)

[71] Stephan Aarsol, *A Federally Funded Venture Capital Program Would Revitalize Entrepreneurs and the Economy* (Washington Post, August 2, 2013)

- Once funded, each entrepreneur has the opportunity to go through a month-long startup boot camp
- Each entrepreneur is assigned an account oversight manager for transparency, and (s)he gains access to a low-cost team of resources (patent attorneys, accountants, etc.) during the initial startup. The U.S. government gets an equity position in exchange for its investment (a la venture capitalists).
- Cash the government out at harvest (commercial deployment for, say, three years), and the winners will make the program self-funded (and very likely profitable) over the long term.

Mr. Kiisel disagrees with Mr. Aarsol's proposed use of the government to provide funding, even with the help of universities to determine the winners of the pitch competitions. Kissel says that it should be The Market which decides who survives and who doesn't. And while that may ultimately be true over the longer term, universities have greater research capabilities and statistical knowledge of current market conditions than does the government. The schools can be arbiters of who gets the money. The federal government simply acts as the fiscal risk taker, with a view towards longer-range risk absorption. The schools and the government can determine the economic risk factors and develop a reasonable Return on Investment to reimburse the government for the risks it takes in funding each enterprise. The allocation of risk can, in fact, be based on a public policy decision regarding the types of businesses we want to support.

The determination of the types of business enterprises worthy of public support can be the product of a National Economic Priorities Board (NEPB), founded along lines similar to its counterpart in Japan in the 1950s and 1960s. The idea behind an NEPB is simple: we need to determine in what direction our country's economy needs to go, and make socio-political decisions on how to get there.

For the neoliberals, of course, this proposal would cause them to suffer from an apoplectic fit. They would argue that The Market should determine what is and what isn't worth pursuing, and government should just get out of the way and let economic forces make the decision.

The problem, of course, is that The Market does not, in fact, work in a vacuum. Laws, rules, regulations, the tax code, all reflect policy decisions that reflect policy judgments made by legislatures at the time the laws were enacted.

The real need, ultimately, is that we must educate people into avoiding the "silo mentality," wherein they think that individual decisions work best, and society be damned. Neither do we want a purely collectivist imprint on our economy. Socially-responsible capitalism provides us with a healthy balance between individual desires and social needs. Without that balance, we wind up with billionaires and the impoverished class, and an almost nonexistent Middle Class.

Individual creativity, hard work, and a constructive attitude should be well rewarded. Unfortunately, The Market is not structured to make the decision of who should be given a chance to start a business. The Market predicates its decisions on risk evaluation, but since that risk evaluation does not factor in greater social needs, it is virtually impossible to find venture capitalists who are willing to give a new, creative, but untried business an opportunity to show what it can do.

Yes, there's "Shark Tank," but for every contestant there are probably 10,000 applicants who don't even get a "thank you" e-mail. Venture capitalists do not generally provide new businesses with the opportunity to take the ball and run with it. A greater risk taker is necessary, and that risk taker should be the federal government. This is because, in a rational society, there is a greater social good to be realized by spreading the risk around so that individual or corporate investors do not bear the entire risk of loss. In our present situation, angel investors and venture capitalists tend to be so risk averse that they are unwilling to put money into a startup unless it's a "sure thing," which seldom exists in the real world.

Under Aarsol's proposal, the use of federal funding, coupled with gatekeeping by academic institutions to sift through applicants' proposals, would tend to bring out the best of the best and enhance the chances of business success. Yes, there will be some failures, but the division between the funding source and the proposals' screeners means that the internalized fear of loss of money does not create an excessively conservative view of proposals.

Additionally, the sum of money involved ($3 billion) is so trivial compared with what the federal government ~~wastes~~ spends in other areas (the military comes to mind), that it is, relatively speaking, chump change. It goes without saying that there will be plenty of analytics to help the academics and government determine (A) who among the universities has the best record in picking successful applicants, and (B) what types of businesses produce the best ROI for the government. Quantitative analysis will help to refine the processes of screening and selecting applications for government grants and this feedback will improve the government's profitability in administering this program.

Returning to Japan, South Korea, and China, the governments there enacted trade and industrial development policies that were based on the idea of protecting and building industries and markets by using tariffs, import quotas, export restrictions, and providing subsidies to industries that needed extra help with research and development. The creation of the equivalents of a National Economic Priorities Board in each of these countries helped to formulate coherent strategies for R&D; industrial support by way of taxes; transportation policies; and rules and regulations governing how the supported companies were to run their businesses.

Were these policies geared towards protecting the Japanese, South Korean, and Chinese economies? Absolutely. Did they work? Unquestionably. Was centralized planning the be-all and end-all of economic development? Of course not---but it worked much better than the completely individualized and disorganized method employed in the United States, and the fact that these economies have demonstrated such profound growth over the last couple of generations suggests that our much-vaunted economic free-for-all is not, in fact, solving the problems we have been experiencing since the days of Ronald Reagan's presidency.

Now, Pres. Trump is unilaterally launching tariffs in a ham-handed way, without properly negotiating or displaying the slightest degree of cultural sensitivity, thus alienating allies around the world. However, the idea behind the use of tariffs and related trade policies had great success throughout much of our history, and, when used with substantially revised tax policy, and funding of startups, could provide America with a major resurgence of its manufacturing base. The key, of course, is proper communication of our underlying premises and being aware of what each trading partner's needs are. To simply impose tariffs without a period of negotiation is not conducive to success, and that's where Trump is wrong. The idea, however, of returning to what worked for so long is not bad; it simply needs to be executed properly.

It would be worth pointing out, then, that the relatively small investment that would be required by the U.S. government in helping to "seed the ground" would likely produce significant, widespread benefits in creating jobs; stimulating new industries and strengthening markets; and broadening our tax base. These are benefits worth pursuing. They were achieved by Japan, South Korea, and China; there is no reason why they could not be realized by the U.S.

CHAPTER 18
WANT HAPPINESS? TRY SOME *HYGGE*.

The World Happiness Report (2019) came out recently. Not surprisingly, a Scandinavian country (in 2019 and 2018, Finland) was reported as the happiest country in the world. For each year since its inception, the WHR reported that countries such as Iceland, Norway, Sweden, Denmark, and Finland were always in the Top 10 (usually the Top 5). The data differences among these Top 5-10 countries were so small that any one of them could easily have vaulted into the top position.

This annual report was first published in 2012 as an outgrowth of the United Nations Sustainable Development Solutions Network and primarily uses data from the Gallup World Poll. The idea behind the annual publication is to help measure improvements in the quality of life in countries around the world, and to help frame public policies that may improve the lives of citizens in each country. The Gallup World Poll questionnaire measures 14 areas within its core questions: (1) business & economic, (2) citizen engagement, (3) communications & technology, (4) diversity (social issues), (5) education & families, (6) emotions (well-being), (7) environment & energy, (8) food & shelter, (9) government and politics, (10) law & order (safety), (11) health, (12) religion and ethics, (13) transportation, and (14) work.

From these 14 areas, there were six key variables that revealed improvements or degradations in countries' Happiness results:

A) GDP
B) Healthy Life Expectancy
C) Social Support
D) Freedom to Make Life Choices
E) Generosity
F) Corruption

In the current version of the WHR,[72] the theme was heavily skewed towards the question of migration, a topic of great concern around the globe for many reasons: global climate change; war/violence in the source countries; stagnant/decreasing economic opportunities in the source countries; and disfavorable political/social/religious/cultural affairs in the source countries.

The United States, which has the biggest economy in the world, is in 18th place.

Let us take a look at the reasons why the Scandinavian countries are perpetually on top.

Economics - yes, the Nordic nations are always in the top 20 countries in terms of GDP. However, studies have shown that while money *does* improve happiness, it's true only up to a point. A recent study showed that in America, once income reached $75,000/year, additional earnings did nothing to add to feelings of happiness[73] The authors - who have both separately won the Nobel Prize in economics - suggested: "Perhaps $75,000 is a threshold beyond which further increases in income no longer improve individuals' ability to do what matters most, such as spending time with people they like, avoiding pain and disease, and enjoying leisure."

High Taxes - the Danes pay 51.5% in taxes. They don't call it "paying taxes," but prefer to say that they are "investing in our

---

[72] Helliwell, J., Layard, R., & Sachs, J., *World Happiness Report 2019* (New York: Sustainable Development Solutions Network, 2019)

[73] Kahneman, Daniel and Deaton, Angus, *High Income Improves Evaluation of Life But Not Emotional Well-being* (Proceedings of the National Academy of Sciences of the United States of America, September 21, 2010)

society." When you look at their system of free education, health care, parental support, and many other social benefits, no wonder they don't feel distressed the way Americans do.

Health and Life Expectancy - the Scandinavians spend very little, individually, on health care. This is attributable to the higher tax rates they pay, with the result of free or virtually free health care. They also tend to engage in much more walking, hiking, bicycling, and other forms of physical exercise than we practice here in the United States. Moreover, their diets are much better (more fish, fruits, vegetables, nuts, and less of the fat-laden, carbohydrate-rich "Supersized" portions made popular at certain fast-food restaurant chains). Healthy diets, more exercise, and regular examinations by their doctors lead to a net result of high life expectancies and much healthier lives. In short, healthier, happier lives means more time above ground and less time under it.

Social Support - this covers a wide range of services that might be considered Utopian here in the United States: meaningful family care (12 months off work for a new mother, to help her bond with her baby; three months off work for a new father, to help him bond with his new baby; with their jobs guaranteed to be held while they are on family leave); free education; much greater emphasis on protecting the environment; much lower crime rates and personal safety issues; broad cultural programs (art, music, plays, sports) that attract widespread participation and enjoyment throughout these countries; and a cultural system that favors interpersonal relationships rather than being enslaved by cell phones, video games, virtual reality, and other forms of technological thralldom.

The Danes have a term for their preferred lifestyle: "hygge" (pronounced "hue-guh"), which connotes a sense of being satisfied with what one has; appreciating one's life, including family, friends, co-workers; and enjoying a sense of cozy contentment with various small self-indulgences, e.g., reading a good book with a cup of coffee in a window reading-nook; spending time chatting with friends in a friendly little neighborhood café; enjoying a quiet weekend hike in the mountains.

The Nordic peoples do not follow the high-strung, neurotic pace of life from which we suffer in the United States. When they work, they work hard and with great seriousness, but work does not define their identities, their sense of personhood. They do not engage in "power walks" as they leave their trains/streetcars to get to work; they are not tethered to cell phones in every spare moment; they don't have multi-volume daily/weekly/ monthly planners; they aren't geared towards climbing to the top of Mt. Ambition. In short, as the Danes might say, they want to lead lives that are "hygge," full of contentment with what they have and not a burning desire to be the "King or Queen of the Hill."

In the United States, we have exalted entrepreneurial activities and attitudes, and think that a super-income means we have achieved "success." We have CEOs of corporations that receive incomes that are anywhere from 50 to 500 times the average wages of their workers. By contrast, the CEOs in Scandinavian countries tend to have much smaller wage gaps. Not surprisingly, there is much greater sense of equality and social parity between top executives and their workers.

Human beings have the "comparison gene," and when they see an unjustified gain on the part of one person or group, they naturally tend to feel resentment, envy, and anger. The pay-gap in Norway, Finland, Sweden, Denmark, and Iceland is much smaller than it is elsewhere, with much better labor-management relations---and it reinforces the notion that unrestricted greed is socially unacceptable.

In the United States, people complain about giving workers a "living wage," but they don't complain about the huge tax breaks and mega-salaries given to corporate executives, along with stock options that turn well-paid executives into multimillionaires.

Perhaps with significant social education we could convey the idea that a greater balance between work and life outside of work might have healthy consequences for us as a people and as a nation.

Freedom to Make Life Choices - abortions are available, and without all the hysterical (and hypocritical) "Pro-Life" blubbering seen and heard here in the U.S. In the Scandinavian countries, they are concerned about the quality of life *after* birth; in the U.S., ***pre-birth***

"life" is sacred. But after birth? Good luck with that; as the Republicans would have it, ***you're on your own.***

But it's not only a matter of reproductive rights. People who wish to stay single; to embrace the homosexual lifestyle; to avoid having children; all are given the freedom to live as they choose. Here in America, our Puritanical *morés* still permeate many parts of our culture, and contaminate our so-called commitment to free choice. The "Bible-thumpers," with their rigid views on morality, ironically have the highest rates of divorce and incest in the nation.

And in Scandinavian countries, class, family connections, where you were born, all play *much* smaller roles in determining the kind and quality of life one lives.

Contrast that with the situation in the United States, where class, race, and where you were born all play major parts in determining one's life course. For example, in a substantial investigation into the correlation between racism and income disparities,[74] the author, Thomas Shapiro, and his team of sociologists studied about 200 families in three cities and three suburban areas from 1998 to 2015. Shapiro found that race affected different outcomes in home ownership; accumulation of assets; education; ability to cope with economic hardship; health; ability to plan for retirement; and ability to leave a legacy.

He and his team found that tax codes; banking practices; so-called "race-neutral" retirement plans; educational programs; and housing patterns had very specific, and negative, impacts on people of color compared to their white counterparts. The ability to move from the ranks of the impoverished to the Middle Class was, to a large extent, a function of race and the concomitant socio-economic factors that play a role in social mobility, or the lack thereof.

As stated elsewhere, we have experienced increasing class- and race-based discrimination in America for many years. The reduction in the size of the American Middle Class means that there are fewer

---

[74] Thomas Shapiro, *Toxic Inequality: How America's Wealth Gap Destroys Mobility, Deepens the Racial Divide, and Threatens Our Future* (<u>Basic Books</u>, 2017)

opportunities to move into that group. It bears repeating that the Middle Class is a buffer zone between the impoverished and the wealthy, and the relative lack of that buffer zone increases the likelihood of hostility between the haves and the have-nots.

We suffer from "toxic inequality," where the Scandinavians generally do not. As societies, they do not suffer from the ego drive, the greed, the blind ambition, that compel people here to value money over family; power over integrity; and privilege over social justice.

And, not incidentally, it may very well be that because the Scandinavians generally enjoy far more freedom to make life choices, they experience much more of the joy of life than we do, here in America.

Generosity - the Nordic nations have long-standing traditions of being socially-helpful and generous to their citizens. The sense that taxes are not high, but that citizens are investing in their societies to make them great places in which to live, imbues much of society's views.

These societies are social democracies. They don't have the tradition of "rugged individualism" that characterized much of our earliest days as a country. Perhaps they have a deeper understanding than do we that Man is, as Aristotle put it, "a social animal," and must assure the survival of the group in order to give individuals a chance to survive. A Danish philosopher once put it this way: "good is multiple; evil is individual."

Perhaps that sounds too "collectivist" for American values, but consider this: it is "the lone wolf," the isolated predator, that causes people to instinctively recoil in fear. The rapacious mentality that divides the world into "hunters and prey," with him being "the hunter," has an unnatural aversion to his fellow human beings (and they to him). It is fortunate that even in America the truly wolfish personalities are relatively few; but they nonetheless exist in sufficient quantities to create the misguided belief among many that individualism is of paramount importance, and anything that smacks of people working together and cooperating for the common good is somehow suspect.

Much of this pathological thinking stems from the distorted views and sophistical arguments of Ayn Rand in *The Fountainhead* and *Atlas Shrugged*, which enjoyed great popularity among American right-wing pseudo-intellectuals during the 1950s and 1960s. Her arguments achieved intellectual resonance among those on the right, such as William F. Buckley; Rush Limbaugh; Andrew Breitbart; Laura Ingraham; Michelle Malkin; and, much later, Ann Coulter. Rand's inherently neurotic and selfish world views are the antithesis of thinking in Scandinavia, and reflect a presumption that "society is the enemy of each person." When taken to its logically-absurd conclusion, Rand would posit that we all must serve our own goals and needs, and to hell with Society. Her sociological extensions of Adam Smith's "Wealth of Nations" thinking suggests that only self-interest has any true merit; anything else is nonsense.

The people of Finland, Denmark, Norway, and Sweden certainly remember that during the days of the Nazis it was only when people banded together to fight a common enemy that they had a chance of survival. They remember that, at the end of it all, generosity to each other, and a binding commitment to fostering the common good, are what make a society good and life worth living.

Corruption - a society's allegiance to law and the rules of ethics and morality determine the extent to which it is not corrupt and committed to societal integrity.

The WHR revealed that the Scandinavians strongly value the rules of law and morality, and they do not believe that society is best served when everybody is trying to "beat the system." In fact, the WHR implicitly found that the more people tried to "beat the system," the more corrupt their society was. This is an obvious extension of the notion that the attempted "system beaters" recognize that there is a tremendous gap between the "haves" who control all the power and the "have-nots," who don't.

The WHR asked respondents about their perceptions of "corruption in government" and "corruption within business." Not surprisingly, in countries where government was viewed as an adjunct of business, corruption was deemed high. Likewise, where government strongly regulated business, even if business was deemed inherently tainted, there was a lower perception of corruption.

Here in America, our TV shows and movies have made much ado about the successful con-man who rigs the rules of the game and beats the house. We love movies such as Ocean's 11 (and 12, and 13); we find it fascinating (and deeply appealing) to be the underdog who overcomes all odds and achieves victory over much more powerful forces. Hell, we're *addicted* to those types of films.

While these cinematic adventures are meant, perhaps, to lull us away from the drudgery of our day-to-day lives, the sad reality is that these operations almost always go down in flames, at great cost. Life, in short, does not produce astonishingly great benefits; it usually leads to disasters, and those who foolishly seek "the Golden Fleece" almost always wind up getting fleeced themselves. The underdog, in reality, is almost always outspent; outmaneuvered in the media; subject to the most unfair obstacles in moving forward; and is required to be scrupulously pure at all times, while the crooks at the top of the hill get away, literally and figuratively, with murder.

In the U.S., for the last 45 - 50 years, we have embraced the amorality of ethical relativism and the lack of standards that that philosophy encompasses. The rappers' mantra, "It's all good," originally conveying a tone of defiance in the face of bad circumstances, has now been co-opted by upper middle-class whites who don't want to be subjected to judgmentalism and the implicit moral condemnation they might face when their lives have been viewed and found wanting.

The Swedes, Norwegians, Danes, Finns and Icelanders have often been viewed as judgmental, probably because of their stern Lutheran faith. A common complaint heard from younger people---and not just Americans---is that the Nordic peoples tend to be judgmental as part of their culture. This trait can be off-putting to those who have a "live-and-let-live" attitude towards life.

This attitude of playing by the rules on the part of the Scandinavians means that they have social, political, economic, and cultural patterns that apply to everyone. Corruption, therefore, tends to be much less prevalent in these countries, because the concept of fairness prevents people from taking undue advantage, of securing an unjustifiable benefit not available to others, of being privileged.

Critics of the Swedes and the Danes, especially, argue that they have lower expectations than others; that they are less ambitious than others, and are therefore far more accepting and appreciative of what they get when their expectations are met. There may be a kernel of truth in these generalizations, but, on the other hand, if the people live longer, are healthier, happier, have more meaningful lives, contribute to science, technology, and the arts, and add value to the quality of human life on earth, why not copy it? Who knows, maybe our neuroses could disappear and our own quality of life might just dramatically improve.

PART III
HEALTH, EDUCATION AND THE ENVIRONMENT

CHAPTER 19
MEDICARE FOR ALL

Collectively, the American people have had a fixation on "going it alone," including health care. The problem with this lone-wolf approach is that there are some goods and services which are far better procured on a social basis: environmental protection; education; police and fire; national defense; international relations; and, of course, health services.

There are many on the right wing who attempt to justify a desire to use society's bargaining power as a reflection of a socialist/communist orientation, a collectivist approach that would turn us into a socialist state. This is, of course, absurd, but their anti-social narrative fails to deal with the common-sense questions of what's best: private firemen or a community/municipal fire department? Individual security guards or a city police department? Private, high-cost doctors or decent doctors for whom everyone pays?

The right wingers attempt to argue that the costs of a "Medicare-for-all" system would bankrupt the country. Using bogus figures from questionable (or nonexistent) sources, the anti-Medicare forces argue that we could not afford to provide good medical coverage to every person lawfully resident in our country. They claim that we would run out of money long before we could provide good health care for them. This argument belies the facts.

In his highly-significant 2014 report[75], Dr. Gerald Friedman established that a nonprofit single-payer system based on the principles of the Expanded and Improved Medicare for All Act, H.R. 676, introduced by Rep. John Conyers Jr., D-Mich., and co-sponsored by 45 other lawmakers, would have saved an estimated $592 billion

---

[75] **Prof. Gerald Friedman, Ph.D.,** *Funding H.R. 676: The Expanded and Improved Medicare for All Act – How We Can Afford a National Single-Payer Health Plan in 2014* (Department of Economics, University of Massachusetts, Amherst, 2014)

in 2014. That would have been more than enough to cover all 44 million people the government estimates were uninsured in that year and to upgrade benefits for everyone else.

"No other plan can achieve this magnitude of savings on health care," Friedman said.

Friedman said the savings would come from slashing the administrative waste associated with today's private health insurance industry ($476 billion) and using the new, public system's bargaining muscle to negotiate pharmaceutical drug prices down to European levels ($116 billion).

"These savings would be more than enough to fund $343 billion in improvements to our health system, including the achievement of truly universal coverage, improved benefits, and the elimination of premiums, co-payments and deductibles, which are major barriers to people seeking care," he said.

Friedman said the savings would also fund $51 billion in transition costs such as retraining displaced workers from the insurance industry and phasing out investor-owned, for-profit delivery systems.

Over the next decade, i.e., from 2015 – 2024, the system's savings from reduced health inflation ("bending the cost curve"), thanks to cost-control methods such as negotiated fees, lump-sum payments to hospitals, and capital planning, would amount to an estimated $1.8 trillion.

"Paradoxically, by expanding Medicare to everyone we'd end up saving billions of dollars annually," he said. "We'd be safeguarding Medicare's fiscal integrity while enhancing the nation's health for the long term."

Unfortunately, the Expanded and Improved Medicare for All Act (H.R. 676) did not survive the firestorm of corporate antipathy from insurers, pharmaceutical manufacturers, and venture capital firms with heavy investments in our health care industry.

In September 2017, Senator Bernie Sanders, along with 15 co-sponsors, introduced a Medicare for All bill in the Senate. It was read twice, then referred to the Senate Finance Committee, where it is apparently languishing.

There is substantial support for Medicare for All. According to an April 2017 poll by The Economist/YouGov, 60 percent of the American people want to "expand Medicare to provide health insurance to every American," including 75 percent of Democrats, 58 percent of independents and 46 percent of Republicans.

Why are these common sense proposals repeatedly defeated? As is the case with everything else in America, it's all about money. The billions of dollars of waste in the administration of insurance plans; the inherent inefficiencies in redundant medical bureaucracies; the billions of dollars of compensation paid to the CEOs and other top executives of the big medical groups and hospitals; the venture capital firms; and the huge pharmaceutical companies, all reflect massive financial incentives to keep a broken system completely dysfunctional.

So, at the end of the day, unlike any other major industrialized country, we lack a single-payer universal health care system. Dying parents, children, and other friends and family members lack a means of obtaining decent quality of health care unless they are fabulously wealthy. The average cost for virtually any significant medical procedure or operation is enough to drive people into bankruptcy or incur huge debt.

The disastrous nature of our permanently-broken health care system has led more and more Democrats to advance ideas for publicly funded health care. On April 18, 2018, U.S. Senators Jeff Merkley (D-Ore.) and Chris Murphy (D-Conn.), joined by U.S. Senators Kamala Harris (D-Calif.), Cory Booker (D-N.J.), Tammy Baldwin (D-Wis.), Brian Schatz (D-Hawaii), Jeanne Shaheen (D-N.H.), Martin Heinrich (D-N.M.), Richard Blumenthal (D-Conn.), Tom Udall (D-N.M.), and Kirsten Gillibrand (D-N.Y.), introduced the *Choose Medicare Act* to give every individual who is not already eligible for Medicaid or Medicare the opportunity to enroll in Medicare as an individual or every employer to purchase Medicare for their employees.

Since the beginning of 2018, more and more Democrats are advancing legislation which focuses on Medicare for All or a variation thereof. How they get there varies from bill to bill, of course, but the main point is that the legislative momentum is clearly in favor of protecting Americans' health needs for the first time since Medicare was originally passed.

That's good news, generally speaking, but there are specific areas that need improvement besides the cost of medical care.

In addition to medical examinations; access to pharmaceuticals; options for surgery; and other forms of health care, a number of health care practitioners take a holistic approach and call for treatment modalities that leave the treatment boundaries of medical school.

We have a large number of homeless and mentally-ill people (not necessarily the same folks, obviously) whose presence is more and more widespread throughout the U.S. every year. These people may have psychogenic problems derived from traumas in the home, family, or work places. Others may have problems derived from drug and/or alcohol use and abuse. Still others may suffer from psychological breakdowns reflecting a mix of both.

Whatever the cause, there are certain baseline requirements that must be fulfilled in a decent civil society if we are to provide reasonable access to health for our people.

- Housing – this won't solve all the problems in the world, but it's a great place to start.
- Stable food supplies – people don't usually think right when they are very hungry.
- Medical care – people need to have examinations and, as needed, treatments.
- Mental care – people need to be given mental care as required by their circumstances. Locking them up in jails/prisons does not provide any kind of healing for what ails them.

In an opinion piece in the Huffington Post[76], a panel of health care experts, Elsa Pearson, MPH; Austin Frakt, Ph.D.; and Sandro Galea, M.D., Dr.PH observed the discrepancies in the Greater Boston area's

---

[76] *America Has a Health Care Gap, and Insurance Alone Won't Fix It*, (The Huffington Post, June 23, 2018)

health outcomes between two neighboring counties, including issues of race, income, (un)employment, and other socioeconomic inequalities.

They also compared certain programs in California and in Ohio and the effects those programs had. What they found, not surprisingly, is that when people had housing; regular access to food; less stress in their personal lives and in their neighborhoods; and a sense that people cared for them or their situations they had much better health outcomes. Many times, the cases of asthma, hypertension, diabetes, heart disease, and many other forms of illness were substantially ameliorated when communities invested in holistic health care.

The communities that invested in low-income housing; that provided meal-delivery services; that provided health care services wound up saving on police and jail costs. They also had better outcomes in getting troubled people out of their perpetual-crisis modes and back into living productive lives as contributing members of society.

This doesn't mean that the people on the subway or sleeping on a bus bench, having arguments with imaginary enemies, will necessarily be ready to take on a job as an executive of a retail chain store. They need psychiatric help, and may need long-term institutional living, but they won't get that in the local or state jails or prisons.

In California, we used to have acceptable---not great, but acceptable---mental institutions. Then, in 1967 Ronald Reagan took office as the Governor of California. Seeing that the number of patients in the State's mental hospitals had decreased to 22,000, Reagan used that decline as justification to dramatically reduce the budget for the Department of Mental Hygiene, even though reports showed that hospitals were well below recommended staffing levels.

The same year, Reagan signed the *Lanterman-Petris-Short Act*, the so-called patients' Bill of Rights, which prevented people from being involuntarily incarcerated in mental institutions, or for indefinite periods of time. Unfortunately, the care for the mentally ill outside of the state hospitals was woefully inadequate. As a result, within a year after the passage of the *Lanterman-Petris-Short Act*, studies showed that the number of mentally ill people entering into state and local jails had doubled in many cases.

Since then, and especially with the advent of the returning Vietnam veterans who suffered from Post-Traumatic Stress Disorder, we have seen a massive increase in the number of mentally disturbed folks who are homeless. Many of them have indulged in self-medication on alcohol and/or drugs, with the result that their brains have been fried and they have no likely destinations to get help.

Even the younger people who have never been involved with the military have been exposed to many types of drugs, some of which can dramatically damage cognitive functions. These people have wound up living hallucination-based lives and literally cannot think clearly or function normally.

So, what do we do about these people?

We certainly cannot allow the problem of increasing homelessness and craziness to continue. Apart from the immorality of letting our fellow humans languish in their misery, there are the practical concerns based on public safety and public order, which is how unpleasant it is to exist in a society with numerous "wack-jobs" on the streets, who live in tents, defecate in public, hassle people for spare change, sing songs on the subways or street corners, and otherwise call attention to themselves and their situations.

People have needs. Healthy people will usually take constructive steps to fulfill those needs by getting an education; obtaining a job; starting a family; and becoming a productive member of society. Unhealthy people will engage in anti-social behavior, such as inappropriate communications; living in conditions of squalor and misery; panhandling; public use and/or sale of drugs; getting involved in public disputes; committing petty (and not-so-petty) crimes; and generally making a mess out of their lives, which messes spill over into the common weal, since they can't look after themselves.

Yes, it's a terrible situation. Yes, we wish it weren't here and that we didn't have to deal with it. Yes, it will cost money to fix---a lot of it.

But:

- If we can spend billions of dollars on aircraft carriers
- If we can pay for military expenditures for new and amazing weaponry
- If we can allow corporate taxes to be reduced to bargain-basement rates

Then why, for God's sake, can't we help alleviate the problems of our poor, befuddled, bedrugged brothers and sisters who need a hand and/or someone professional to look out for and take care of them?

Either we will take care of these people or our social decadence will continue, and we will simply be another "s***hole country" about which President Trump complained. Do we really want that, or do we have enough pride and self-respect (and a sense of morality) to do what's right and to help the afflicted among us?

During the last several years, America's average life-expectancy has declined, and the rate of suicide has increased, all because of the dramatic increase in the amount of opioids being prescribed by doctors for pain-management and "nerve conditions." People who can't get opioids wind up taking heroin.

Studies have shown that when communities *care* about the quality of life for their afflicted members, then health outcomes dramatically improve.

The secret to success in this regard is *attitude*. We have to realize, at long last, that we simply cannot afford to take an insular approach to the world. We cannot automatically assume that someone else will take care of the problems we are facing. If we do not adopt an attitude of personal responsibility then we will wind up living very unhappy, very frustrated lives.

There used to be a widespread phrase, "Let George do it." Well, "George" had so many loads of work dumped on his back that it broke, and "George" can't do anything anymore. So the operative phrase, now, has turned into "If it's to be, it must start with me."

Obviously, this does not mean that you have to shoulder the entire load; that would be absurd and suicidal. But it ***does*** suggest that personal responsibility requires that if you see an important problem that's too big for you to handle alone, you must seek help from others who might be similarly affected, who just might be persuaded to help.

This is the situation with our health care situation. As things stand now, we have many needs, and too few hands. My mother used to quote a great phrase: "Many hands make light of much work." Let's see if we can start a gathering of hands.

The universal phrases are "let's build affordable housing" and "get these people decent homes," but the problem can be summarized by one word: NIMBY (Not In My Back Yard). People who have worked hard to get into a good home in a good neighborhood do not want to confront formerly homeless people. They do not want to have to deal with different cultural values and perspectives. Mothers are afraid for the safety of their children. There are many social and psychological barriers to getting the homeless integrated into the larger society. This was, and to a large extent still is, the principal obstacle to racial integration and integration of the schools. "White flight" was, and still is, a significant factor in trying to integrate housing developments. Notwithstanding the superficial homilies about living together in peace and harmony, the fact remains that there are many, many parts of the country where racial integration in housing is more a dream than a reality.

Imagine, then, the difficulties in convincing normal people to allow communal housing for the borderline mentally ill in their communities. Obviously, massive social and cultural education would be necessary, and, naturally, there would have to be reasonable assurances that the more seriously affected mentally-challenged people would be kept in institutions, for their own safety and the safety of the larger community.

But the key ingredient in overcoming these obstacles is a concerted pattern of education, started by political will of leaders who understand that we cannot keep kicking the can down the road. The foregone conclusion that we will always have the poor with us (and the concomitant belief that we will always have crazy people with us, too) has caused too many people to throw up their hands in despair and ask: "I'm just one person; what can I do?"

As the title of this book suggests, the answer is "Plenty!"

There are three practical steps you can take.

1) Become educated about the conditions of homelessness and mental illness.
2) Talk to friends, family, neighbors, co-workers who may be affected by the situation. Form "action groups" who are willing to join forces in talking to people in City Hall about programs that could help the homeless and/or the mentally ill.
3) Start pressuring your elected representatives---your employees---to take positive actions, and not merely suggest yet more studies that simply gather dust on a bookshelf, otherwise your representatives will soon find themselves out of a job.

And remember: "If it is to be, it must start with me!"

CHAPTER 20
GET A DEGREE, GET A JOB, GET A LIFE

From the 1950s up until 2010, the mantra was "get a degree, get a job, and then you can settle down and have a good life." In today's society, so much has changed that this life-plan tautology is simply no longer true.

Setting aside the dramatically-altered job landscape of the late 20-teens, and the radical shifts in lifestyle choices, the foundational statement was and still is the need for a "good education." Many thoughtful people no longer agree on what that term means, however, and with so many options before us, it's hard to be confident in making the right choice.

Traditionally, when there was a substantial manufacturing capacity in our economy, a person not interested in college could graduate from high school and have an opportunity to work in skilled trades. Being part of a union meant that technical training would be available, and there would be the ability to go from apprentice, to journeyman, to master, with increased pay and the satisfaction of achieving tangible results, of "making a good life" for his family.

As a member of a union, a worker had stable working conditions, a steady paycheck, and a certain life-direction that gave continuity to his family. There would be family tradition, largely associated with work, and a sense of community based on working in the same plant, living in the same neighborhood, going to the same school, attending the same church.

Social organizations in the communities where there was commonality of work, school, and worship focused on reinforcing the values associated with each sub-group, but they also reinforced the greater community's values of belonging, of group identity, of being part of an extended family. The people you saw at work were the same ones at the Little League games, watching their sons play baseball. Those were the same people who went to your church, or one very similar to it. They were the same folks with whom you went fishing. And they were the same people who worked in your factory.

In short, under those conditions, there was a tremendous reinforcement of "us," and anyone not part of "us" was necessarily part of "them," almost always perceived as a threat. On a subconscious, "reptile brain" level, we thought: "Us good, Them bad."

In the 1950s and especially in the 1960s, America's economy started to experience a transition to more knowledge-based jobs. Advances in computational abilities, more engineering jobs, sophisticated work tied into our military and space programs as well as infrastructure projects, all required more education than was available at the high school level.

Right after World War II, millions of returning U.S. servicemen took advantage of the G.I. Bill and were able to receive educational support in college. The program continued in its original up through July 25, 1956, and was revised several times since then. Countless engineers, technicians, and others in the fields of science, technology, and engineering derived their educations because of the G.I. Bill, which profoundly and beneficially impacted America's economy and place in the world.

More importantly than merely developing technical skills, however, the value of properly structured higher education lay in its ability to help students learn how to think critically; to examine two or more conflicting thoughts; to weigh and make decisions about differing facts; to gather and analyze data; and to assess the pros and cons of various courses of action that might present themselves in real life. This was not merely decision-tree analysis, but the ability to impart values onto knowledge, and to make wise choices based on values-based learning.

In a manner of speaking, a "liberal arts" education could provide a student with the ability to engage in critical thinking, to undergo a thoughtful review and analysis of <u>The Great Books of the Western World</u>, as envisioned by the University of Chicago President, Robert Hutchins, and his colleague, Mortimer Adler. Its goal was to produce a wise person, with enough insight into the Western World and his own role therein, to be a mature, productive member of society, not merely as a working automaton, but as someone with a developed philosophy of life and an understanding of his role in society.

This type of education was, for a time in the 1960s, a goal in many colleges and universities, but two distinct counter-trends served to thwart it before it became a universal part of America's post-high school education program. These trends were:

1) Meta-ethical relativism, and
2) Corporate sponsorship/coopting of the education process, starting in elementary schools.

"It's Your Thing"

Starting in the mid-to-late 1960s and continuing thereafter, there was a convergence of several forces in society which led to dramatic upheavals in both social and educational goals and values. One was the civil rights movement, which arguably reached a tipping point at the time of the assassination of Dr. Martin Luther King, Jr. on April 4, 1968. Another was the anti-war movement, which in 1967 and 1968 was growing dramatically stronger. Yet another was the so-called "Hippie Movement" of the period from "The Summer of Love" in 1967 and continuing to the time of the Woodstock music festival in August 1969.

With the civil rights movement, and the calls for increased black militancy made by the Black Panthers; the Student Nonviolent Coordinating Committee; the Students for a Democratic Society; and the Weather Underground, young black leaders felt that it was incumbent for a new spirit of black pride to permeate political, social, and educational life. As a result, there were massive successful calls for Black History Month, the celebration of Dr. King's birthday, and for Black Studies majors programs to be instituted in colleges and universities throughout the country.

In popular black R&B music, there was "Do Your Thing" (1968, Charles Wright and the Watts 103rd Street Rhythm Band) and "It's

Your Thing" (1969, The Isley Brothers). And with the mixture of the (mostly) white Hippies and their black brothers and sisters, the phrase "Do your thing" was a widespread affirmation of the right of people to make free choices in their lives. It was as popular among younger people as "Aloha" was among tourists in Hawai'i.

Related in some key respects to the civil rights movement was the anti-war fervor of young people. Born at the end of World War II up to 1952, Baby Boom males had to register for the draft. They were called to fight in what many believed was an illegal war in Vietnam, and lots of them felt that the sons of the wealthy were exempt from military duty (due to bone spurs?) while the poor, especially people of color, were given a gun and shipped off to jungles to fight (and die) in a war in which none of them believed.

Indeed, some of Dr. King's strongest rhetoric was directed not only at the goal of achieving an end to racism, but also the quest for a peaceful country where leaders' decisions were not made based on subservience to the military-industrial complex, but on allegiance to what was socially, politically, and economically just.

Many of the tactics and strategies of the civil rights leaders were followed by the leaders of the anti-war movement: petitions, sit-ins, political rallies, mass protests. The mind-set of the anti-war proponents was radically different than that of people during World War II. In World War II, there were clearly identifiable enemies (Hitler, Mussolini, Tojo), and it was not hard to become patriotically charged up with the notion of fighting the Nazis, the *fascistas*, or the Imperial Japanese military.

By contrast, in Vietnam, American leaders had become involved in the early 1950s when they attempted to prop up France's Indochinese empire. By the time of President John Kennedy's assassination in November 1963, American forces had already seen how strong the army of the North Vietnamese was, even though they lacked the sophisticated equipment and seemingly unending supplies of the Americans. One thing the North Vietnamese had in their favor was a burning desire for independence, and this energized them from 1945, when Ho Chi Minh started his nationalist fight against the French, up to the day the last American left their country, some 30 years later.

With this dramatically different attitude, the anti-war forces formed alliances with civil rights groups in the black, brown, and Native American communities in order to gain political power and influence in challenging America's military venture half-way around the world. These alliances were frightening to the Southern Democrats as well as the Republicans living in the suburbs and other predominantly white areas, because the joining of forces of whites, blacks, browns, and reds appeared to be some sort of evil transformation of America from what they thought was an all-white haven to an amalgam of….<u>others</u>….who would threaten their values, their traditions, their entire way of life.

Finally, the advent of the Hippies in San Francisco's Haight-Ashbury District and many other parts of the country in the late 1960s represented a further dramatic change from the values and traditions of the conservative parts of society. With the widespread use of psychedelic drugs and marijuana, and with the now-universal availability of the birth-control pill, the Hippies' slogan of "Sex, Drugs, and Rock 'n' Roll" became a reality. "Free sex" was a rallying cry at many of the music festivals and clearly was enhanced by the easy availability of drugs which naturally reduced judgment and self-restraint. On top of everything else, many of the Hippies were runaways who were attracted to the so-called free-and-easy lifestyle that were embodied in the songs of the day. Many of those runaways may have had serious psychological disturbances to begin with, and the lifestyle probably just made matters worse.

The biggest musical acts---the Beatles, the Rolling Stones, Jimi Hendrix, Santana, Eric Clapton, among many others---had the *panache* that attracted their fans to the Hippie world.

The hallmark advertisement for the alternative lifestyle was the musical "Hair: The American Tribal Love-Rock Musical."

In this musical, all three elements discussed above had great currency and were the calling cards of the young people of the day. Civil rights (the end of racism), peace (an end to the Vietnam War), and harmony (the Hippie lifestyle) were extolled to the singing and dancing audiences throughout the world and, for a brief moment, gave progressives a sense of hope and a vision of a better world.

By the end of the 1960s, however, President Nixon and his Vice President, Spiro T. Agnew, had rallied their Republican base and conservative Southern Democrats to oppose civil rights, peace, and the alternative lifestyle. By the year 1972, it was clear to corporations and to schools of higher education that free speech and free thought were subject to conservative control.

Since there was still some degree of academic freedom in the early 1970s, schools started to attract professors with backgrounds that would attract students who had been exposed to the popular ideas of a few years before, but who wouldn't actually advocate that students *do* something.

Accordingly, many of the teachers' instructions contained references and comments about meta-ethical relativism, the notion that there is no objective right or wrong and everything is "just a matter of opinion."

Critics of ethical relativism claim that it fails because it rejects basic premises of discussions on morality, or because it cannot arbitrate disagreement. Many critics have suggested that ethical relativists essentially take themselves out of any discussion of normative morality, since they seem to be rejecting an assumption of such discussions: the premise that there are right and wrong answers that can be discovered through reason. Practically speaking, such critics will argue that meta-ethical relativism may amount to moral nihilism, or else it is simply incoherent. For those lacking intellectual discipline (or for those whose brains have been fried as the result of ingesting too many drugs), ethical relativism may seem to have a superficial attraction of "live-and-let-live," but it does not withstand any serious scrutiny based on reason.

Many of the Hippies were exposed to Asian religions, whose practices were appealing to those raised in the more rigorous, tightly-defined range of Baptism, Methodism, Lutheranism, or other Protestant sects. Some of the "free-form" religions included chanting, incense, meditation, and other activities that allowed for greater self-expression.

A Zen Buddhist phrase frequently heard among the Hippies was "it's all good." This phrase suggested that all things lead to *nirvana,* a state of freedom from the cycle of birth, misery, death, and reincarnation (*samsara*). When we learn from the bad causes we make and thereafter avoid the bad effects that come from those causes, over time we will be released from *samsara*. We will be "blown-out" and achieve a state of *anatta*, a condition of having no soul. This is the ultimate goal in Buddhism, regardless of whether one follows the religion's *Theraveda*, *Mahayana*, or *Vajrayana* practices.

Western theological thinkers are obviously not in accord with these beliefs. Practitioners of all three Abrahamic religions (Judaism, Christianity, and Islam) believe in the human soul. As such, the Hippies who espoused "it's all good" endorsed an axiom of religion that did not comport with a belief in the soul, not anything that would satisfy Western religious standards.

Suppose, however, that one is an atheist and does not believe in the existence of a soul. What then?

One does not have to believe in the soul in order to have moral principles, and to be able to resolve disagreements as to "right" and "wrong." Critics of ethical relativism argue that "morality is the application of reason to human affairs, and ethics is the application of reason to human motivations." (Thomas A. Murray, Jr., Director of the U.S. Atomic Energy Commission 1950-1957.) Those who believe that morals and ethics are matters of opinion, depending on the group to which you belong, have eliminated reason from the discussion of right and wrong, and of the development of standards that should govern human behavior.

"We Don't Want Critical Thinkers 'Round Here!"

Corporations are largely the economic masters in our economy. As was the case during the days of slavery in Egypt, Greece, Rome, the Middle Ages, and in America, masters would not tolerate people who questioned authority and the decisions of those in positions of power. So, too, in America corporations do not countenance true free speech or challenges to the exercise of corporate powers.

How can corporations assure themselves of minimal intrusions in the corporate decision-making and executive processes?

The solution began at the local level in the 1950s and 1960s. In smaller municipalities, school boards did not always have a local version of John Dewey waiting to run for office. Candidates needed money. More often than not, the local school boards had few resources for school programs. The solution was simple: in exchange for corporations providing campaign funds for tractable candidates, and money for school programs, the candidates would have to comply with their corporate masters' wishes.

As a result, throughout rural and small-town America for the last 50-60 years, corporations were able to get pliable candidates elected to offices on the school boards and in school administration. Academic agendas changed. Facts and "faith" soon assumed equivalency, and then matters of science such as evolution became considered optional or subject to equal treatment.

Multiply this process hundreds and thousands of times over the years; have corporations encourage/mandate the use of textbooks that did not examine the contributions of African-Americans, Latinx-Americans, Asian-Americans, and Native Americans to the development of our country; teach people a completely skewed way of learning; teach them to take and pass tests (and to quickly forget what they learned right after the tests); and then get them hooked on the latest toys and gadgets; and it will be no wonder that we have people who don't know their geography, history, social sciences, political situation, or culture.

These are people capable of spending eight or ten hours a day on the phone but haven't read a book on their own; who have been "Keeping Up With the Kardashians," but don't know the names of their city council(wo)man, State Senator, or U.S. Senator; who could talk about sports for hours, but could not intelligently argue and coherently express their opinion for or against a single political point.

Are they grist for the corporate mill? You bet. Will their corporate masters be happy to bring them on board? Oh, yeah. Will they be able to think critically and determine what corporations are doing to harm the environment? Of course not. Will they fight for what's right and challenge corporate power? Not on your life.

With corporate greed and unbridled spending of private money on political campaigns, it is hardly surprising that politicians have enacted laws that allow for dramatically-increased costs for attending colleges and universities. The creation of a student-loan industry, coupled with the inability to get a discharge of student debt if a former student files for bankruptcy protection, means that the cost of education is out of line for the average person. As stated in Chapter 15, student loans have risen to reflect the higher cost of education, and the cost of education is rising far faster than the salaries designed to pay for it.

✳✳✳

As discussed in Chapter 18, the Scandinavian countries allow people to attend school for free. Yes, they pay higher taxes, but they enjoy a well-educated, sophisticated populace who can and do think critically, who can consider and discuss multiple points of view, and make informed decisions that help improve their societies.

Being educated is not necessarily a guarantor of wisdom, but wisdom comes to those who learn to think, weigh different factors, and determine probable outcomes. An educated person is more likely to learn how to think, compare and contrast than someone stuck on the phone or playing video games for hour after hour every day.

"Happy is the man who finds wisdom, and the man who gains understanding" (Prov. 3:13).

Ultimately, we should seek wisdom, for it is with wisdom that our lives become full of meaning. That process should include education, and education should be deemed an essential human right to which every person in our society should be entitled. In today's society, many students obtain the money for their schooling by taking out student loans. Clearly, student loans were and are a massive exercise in wallet-vacuuming, engineered by greedy financiers who have lobbied Congress for exemptions from the protections of the bankruptcy law, part of a private educational establishment that focuses its efforts on fleecing students with false promises of "great jobs" that can "easily be had with a degree" from this or that school. The public universities, too, have joined the process of convincing students to pay exorbitant fees for tuition, books, pre- and post-registration costs of one sort or another. Student loans are simply not an economically-viable option for most folks, yet, more than ever, people need to go to college. This is, arguably, a universal need.

How Do We Pay for Universal Education Through College?

Here's how we do it. We swap the Dept. of Defense and the Dept. of Education budgets for 25 years, then take a look at the results. [Naturally, we'd have to dramatically revise our education system to (A) end the frequent changes in educational theories and approaches. Let's find out what works best, domestically and internationally, then try it; and (B) stop the long summer vacations and make learning a fun, year-round experience.]

At the end of that period, I bet we'd have the smartest people on the planet, people who could speak multiple languages, code proficiently by the time they reach their early-to-mid-teens, be culturally-attuned to regional cultural centers around the world, and KNOW HOW TO CRITICALLY-THINK. Oh, and by the way, if the armed forces had to fund the purchase of aircraft carriers and other advanced military equipment by holding bake-sales the way schools do when they need money, I bet we'd have far fewer foreign military adventures.

(That would be a benefit to the parents and spouses of military personnel who would not needlessly die to increase the profits of MIC corporations, and would serve to show other countries around the planet that we no longer view ourselves as the world's policeman.)

A state defined by repressive, formal, legal, social controls based on physical force is not necessary in the development of civilization.[77]

Although this idea has a lot to recommend it, we are probably not evolved enough as a nation to accept it, so here's another suggestion, this time from Vermont Senator Bernie Sanders: enact a "speculation tax" that would impose a small tax on Wall St., i.e., on people who trade stocks, bonds, and derivatives. Estimates are that such a tax

---

[77] Elman Service, *Origins of the State and Civilization* (New York, Norton, 1975)

would raise anywhere from $250 billion to $350 billion per year. It would be more than sufficient to cover the costs of universal education in community schools, state colleges and universities. Private, Ivy League schools such as Dartmouth; Brown; Cornell; Princeton; Yale; University of Pennsylvania; Columbia; and Harvard may qualify, but then again much of their attraction lies in how they appeal to people with snobbish attitudes who think that acceptance into one of them signifies superiority of some kind or other. Perhaps that's not a message that necessarily needs to be promoted in this day and age.

Sen. Sanders' proposal did not get enacted, for the same reasons that so many other progressive ideas are doomed in Congress (and in state legislatures): private money is used to fund public functions, and there's a lot of money to be made in our present education racket. While this situation is just one of many that cries out for removing the influence of private money to pay for public requirements, education is of such critical importance that we really need to prioritize a solution for this problem.

The next chapter will discuss the direction our educational system must take if we are to succeed in moving our economy forward in the 21st century. An emphasis on STEM courses is vital if we are to retain our position as an economic leader in the world.

CHAPTER 21
STEM: THE ENVIRONMENTAL DRIVER

These are the four areas in which Americans have been sadly deficient for the last 50 – 60 years. Much of our advances in Science, Technology, Engineering, and Mathematics programs have come from foreigners.

The people who received their college/university educations in the late 1940s up to 1970---mostly white males---did so under the twin motivating forces of free education via the G.I. Bill and the increasing militarization of our economy. The military did not require degrees in English Literature or Comparative Philosophy; instead, the government and the contractors who worked for the government wanted people who were good in the areas under STEM. People who were comfortable with slide rules; understood math, science, engineering, and/or technology; and had the mental discipline to pursue these topics were hired in record numbers. The economy demanded these skills; the companies doing the hiring weeded out those who didn't have them; and those who chose not to, or couldn't, develop them got jobs as teachers or in second-rate occupations.

The late Baby Boom and Generation X parents loved the anything-goes attitudes that came from the late 1960s and fostered an attitude of academic freedom (tied into the ethical-relativism previously discussed). Students who did poorly in math or related hard-sciences in early grades were encouraged to try out soft-sciences (e.g., sociology; economics; psychology) where intellectual rigor and discipline were not necessarily required in the same way they were in the hard sciences, which dealt with objective facts and the scientific method.

The lack of intellectual discipline has led to an astonishing decline in American students' academic achievements over the last 50 years or so. We rank appallingly low on STEM scores, and it is not surprising now to see that the vast majority of STEM students in American schools come from China, India, Russia, and Iran.

The need for STEM program improvements is based on the fact that the world is tremendously interconnected. If we are to economically compete in the global marketplace, it will be vital to restore our ability to innovate in various fields, especially biology, pharmaceuticals, and advanced manufacturing technologies.

A major problem in American education is the lack of significant numbers of teachers in the STEM disciplines. Another problem is the perception that a STEM graduate works harder and earns less money. A further obstacle in the U.S. is that people focus on things that "look glamorous," so they go into high-knowledge, high-cost fields (law, medicine, advanced degrees in business).

However, what many people don't realize is the fact that STEM never sleeps. There will always be a need for innovations in science; technology; engineering; and mathematics. A majority of Americans didn't understand that, as Arianna Huffington said, "We used to make things; now, we just make things up." This is especially true in law, finance and business, where we shuffle papers, use fancy words, and pretend to be "Masters of the Universe."

If we want to resume our place as economic leaders in the world, we are going to have to dramatically increase interest in, and provide financial benefits for, STEM students and graduates. Likewise, we have to increase the prestige of being a STEM graduate; in foreign countries, having a strong background in STEM is equivalent to going to an Ivy League school in the U.S., while here, STEM graduates are viewed as nothing more than moderately-paid "white-collar *braceros*."

A solution to this problem of low interest in STEM can be based on political will to develop education programs to show people *why* STEM is so important. Of special importance will be a multi-media program starting in the early years of schooling, but also public service announcements by celebrities showing how a STEM education is the key to personal and social success. You might think this is naïve and could not possibly work, but think of this reality: if we start creating jobs in different parts of our economy---infrastructure, conversion from a hydrocarbon to a renewable-energy economy, development of new technologies---then we have a chance to say "If you want to work, you'd better learn about STEM"

We used to value people with brainpower and the discipline to become scientists, technicians, engineers, or mathematicians. No, not all of them were going to start up businesses, or become the darlings of venture capitalists, but they were the people who explored ideas that might become products or services; who might be the technicians, engineers, or mathematicians who designed them and built them; and who might figure out the fundamental mathematical laws that would govern whole spheres of interesting and potentially major new technologies and industries.

The Environment is the Driver for Educational Change

Since our environment is being objectively threatened as the result of global climate change, it will be vital, as a matter of survival as a species, to formulate new ways to live, farm, travel, communicate, produce energy, develop and properly use water, deal with migrating populations, protect endangered species, and modify many other aspects of our lives.

We will have to avoid needless warfare and violent conflicts throughout the world; learn to cooperate regardless of differences in race/ethnicity, religion, country of origin, gender, or sexual preferences; and figure out methods for communicating in mutually-respectful and effective ways.

These changes require massive changes in the underlying aspects of our economy. The hydrocarbon-based economy of the United States is simply placing an unsustainable environmental burden on the world's climate. With about 4% of the world's population, the United States generates about 25% of the carbon dioxide emitted into the atmosphere, as well as the carbon dioxide which sinks into the oceans and dramatically changes the complex body of ocean-atmosphere interactions.[78] Tragically, President Trump has withdrawn the United States from the Paris Climate deal entered into in December 2015.

Thus, the world's biggest polluter has walked away from its responsibilities as a member of mankind.

Now, I do not for a moment believe that STEM proficiency will automatically render us capable of remediating the problem of global climate change. In Chapter 2, I referred to the Myth of Scientific Supremacy, discussed by Steward Udall in his book *The Quiet Crisis*. The notion that "science trumps all problems" has been unequivocally proved to be false. We have developed countless technologies with harmful or disastrous effects because we could, but without asking if we should.

Wisdom is essential in the renaissance of STEM in America. We will need the technological prowess of STEM capabilities, but must blend those capabilities with the wisdom of ethical considerations and the use of morally-justifiable values in our decision-making processes.

STEM graduates will necessarily assume greater roles in helping to develop and deploy new technologies that sequester carbon dioxide in the atmosphere and in the oceans; that develop new technologies for alternative energy production and storage; that will produce new ideas and technologies for infrastructure improvements to roads, bridges, lighting systems, waterways; that will produce new technologies for urban development and home construction; that will produce new methods of transportation that will leave no net carbon footprints; that will produce orders of magnitude more data inputs (meaning that we will need more data scientists than engineers by the year 2020); that will lead to even more promising (or threatening?) versions of artificial intelligence; and that will lead to new and exciting advances in medical care.

These, and many other areas of enhanced human activities, will necessarily mean that we will have to shift our educational focus and

---

[78] *Carbon Dioxide Information Analysis Center* (Oak Ridge National Laboratory, 2014)

social attitudes away from "glamour gigs" and more towards the practical fields described above, towards solving real problems that affect our lives and those of people around the world.

Again, STEM courses *must* receive priority attention. Teachers in STEM topics must be recruited with a combination of substantial pay increases; academic, business, and social support; and political leadership that will return us to "making things, instead of making things up."

Values-free economic activity since the end of World War II has led to three generations of "making a dying" instead of "making a living." We have treated the environment as a vast reservoir from which to extract resources without considering the long-range impact on the air we breathe, the water we drink, the soils we farm, and the oceans in which we fish. This woeful approach to the environment must stop NOW if we are to have a fighting chance to survive as a species.

Use the S.T.A.R. System to Properly Educate Students

Some psychologists have developed a quadrature of human personality characteristics. They call this the S.T.A.R. system.

It stands for S(tructure), T(echnical), A(ction), R(elationship). It is vitally-important to understand the personality characteristics, and to remember that we each have a principal and a secondary part of these characteristics to reflect our personalities. These characteristics are usually well-established by the time we are in our mid-adolescent years, i.e., 14 – 17. Here are the qualities of each personality type:

STRUCTURE

- STABILITY
- DUTY
- PREDICTABILITY
- CREDENTIALS
- RESPONSIBILITY
- TITLES
- STRUCTURE
- DEPENDABILITY
- BELONGING
- TRADITION
- RULES
- OWNERSHIP

TECHNICAL

- KNOWLEDGE & LEARNING
- SELF-MASTERY
- UNIVERSAL TRUTHS
- INSIGHT
- COMPETENCE
- CONCEPTS
- LOGICAL CONSISTENCY
- PROGRESS
- INTELLIGENCE
- UNDERSTANDING
- THE LARGER PICTURE
- ACCURACY

ACTION

- FREEDOM OF ACTION
- ADAPTABILITY
- SPONTANEITY
- ACTION — NOW
- MAKING AN IMPACT
- BEAUTY
- STIMULATION
- EXCITEMENT
- VARIETY
- OPPORTUNITY
- OPTIONS & CHOICES
- PASSION

RELATIONSHIP

- EMPATHIC RELATIONSHIPS
- IDENTITY
- SIGNIFICANCE
- HARMONY
- AUTHENTICITY
- IDEALS
- INVOLVEMENT
- MORALITY
- SELF-ACTUALIZATION
- ETHICS
- COOPERATION
- PERSONAL GROWTH

It is possible to create tests to be administered at the end of the 4th, 7th, and 10th grades that would assess personality types. These tests could and should be used to help guide students into the right types of education programs that would best fit their personality types and allow the optimum development of their skills and interests.

For example, in World War II and in the 1950s, America was largely a "Structure" and "Technical" society. We insisted on order, discipline, status (**Structure**), as well as knowledge, logic, and accuracy (**Technical**). These were qualities necessary to fight the war, and to develop our modern economy based on science and technology.

Starting in the 1960s and continuing thereafter, there was a shift in social priorities, and many of us focused on civil rights, women's rights, peace and harmony, self-actualization, and other empathic qualities (**Relationship**).

By the beginning to mid-1980s, music and other forms of entertainment changed, and, with the advent of "rap" and "hip-hop," America became an "**Action**" society. We emphasized speed, action, athletics, opportunities for minorities, stimulation/excitement. That orientation characterizes us today.

"Action" people are the athletes, the entrepreneurs, the explorers, the risk-takers. They engage in high-speed action (and, of course, make high-speed mistakes---but they don't care). They get things done. Much of what they do is based on ego. An argument can be made that the noticeable increase in Attention-Deficit Disorder is a reflection of our shift into an "Action" society.

A balanced society is much stronger than a country with an overemphasis on one or another personality type. As zoology has taught us, diversity is nature's secret weapon against extinction. If we support each personality type, and give it a venue in which to express itself in a healthy way, we stand a much better chance of growing as a society.

For example, the STEM students typically would come from the Structure and Technical personality types. Look at the qualities of each, and you won't find many poets, writers, or musicians there. But they will produce business, economic, technical, and social systems that will create jobs, new technologies and industries, and create stability. One of the defects in our society over the last couple of generations has been the lack of stability, and it is this insecurity that has precipitated a crisis mentality among many groups.

On the other hand, we need Relationship personalities to create and enhance bonds between differing groups, to foster connections, to imbue our society with a sense of morality and meaning, and return us to pursuing the ideals that made us the "Shining City on the Hill."

Some people love books and studying; others find that working with their hands is fulfilling; still others like creating and overcoming challenges. There can and should be courses designed to fulfill the psychological needs of students so that by the time they are of college age, they can obtain the types of training and education appropriate to their personalities. There is no useful purpose in forcing a garage mechanic to study, contrast and compare the writing styles of William Shakespeare and Sir Francis Bacon. Likewise, an empathetic personality type should not be forced to compete for a position on a varsity football team.

When people are given a chance to do what they enjoy doing, and are most capable of performing, the result is a society where people are more efficient, effective, and fulfilled, and who produce better products and services than those provided under conditions of duress.

The difference between the psychological testing I am proposing versus the testing that found favor among corporations in the 1980s and 1990s lies in the use of the tests. In the corporate environment, the tests would be used to identify potential "troublemakers" and weed them out or place them in positions where they could not do any "harm." In my proposal, using methods advocated by American psychologist B.F. Skinner in his famous novel, *Walden Two*, psychological testing would be used to help educate/train people so that they would be happy and fulfilled in their work and could make their leisure time more pleasurable and satisfying.

Our society is too far out of balance, with an excessive amount of "Action" people in positions of influence and power. My proposal about developing and implementing programs to bring out more STEM students on an expedited basis is essential for survival as a species, and is also necessary, locally, to help enhance personal fulfillment in work and leisure. A balanced society, with more people doing what they enjoy, is a society with strong potential for long-term growth. It reduces the likelihood for conflicts, because happy people who get what they need have fewer motivations to strike out at others.

Racism, xenophobia, homophobia, and misogyny are ultimately the reactions of people who feel threatened and don't have what they feel they need. If the origins of these forms of hatred are explored, it can be seen that there are massive deficits in the haters' lives which promote anti-social attitudes and/or behaviors. Remember the triune brain theory discussed at the beginning of this book? The "reptilian brain" is triggered when primitive threat triggers are pulled. The sense of being threatened declines, however, when the fears that are triggered diminish.

Societal balance tends to reduce those fears, I believe, because of our "compare-and-envy" gene's lessened influence when we see fewer differences between us. This hard-wired tendency on our part to compare ourselves with others and favorably or unfavorably judge our status is reduced when we see little or no difference; big differences, especially when we are on the lower end of the scale, make us feel like we are at a disadvantage. Feeling disadvantaged invokes a whole host of survive-at-any-cost instincts, and starts up the "us versus them" way of thinking.

Thus, a return to societal balance is necessary, and a good way to bring it about is to create conditions of stability which can be achieved through restoring this country to the strong Structure and Technical social type which prevailed from 1945 to 1965. We need to change the nature of the jobs we create, the businesses we run, and the methods we use to test students, followed by academic priorities that provide educational guidance for our children from young ages through college years.

I predict far fewer incidents of hate once we start to implement this system, because the triggers will be dramatically reduced if not eliminated.

CHAPTER 22
INFRASTRUCTURE AND CONVERTING OUR ENERGY SYSTEM

In America for much of the 20th century, we were a great manufacturing power. We were mostly an agricultural society up until World War I, but afterwards we dramatically increased the number and sophistication of our factories. We built and sold so many different types of products, created so many industries, and made massive changes in how our economy ran that a time traveler who traversed the 100 years from 1900 to 2000 would have no idea that he was in the same country.

However, much of our manufacturing was based on dirty means of production. A lot of what we built was produced through degrading our environment, whether through air, water, or soil pollution (and oftentimes all three). The sad reality is that the old phrase "I'm making a living" should really be translated to "I'm making a dying," what with the carcinogens and other deadly pollutants that have pervaded our environment over the years.

Again, the Myth of Scientific Supremacy is just that: a myth. Fixing a broken system is not nearly as easy or effective as preventing its degradation in the first place. What was that old phrase Mom used to say?

"If you don't mess up your room, you don't have to clean it later on."

She was right.

After World War II, we converted our economy from being "maker-minded" to "market-minded," and began crafting advertising techniques modeled on the propaganda used by the Nazis and fascists (and the U.S. government) during World War II. In his famous work on the use of psychology in advertising[79], consumer reporter Vance Packard explored the psychological explorations of advertising agencies into "market research," using supraliminal techniques designed to convince people to buy things they didn't need. In a following book, *The Waste Makers*, Packard revealed the concepts of "planned obsolescence" to create products with artificially short life-spans so that American consumers would buy more and more, and swell the bank accounts of manufacturers.

The problem, of course, is that there's only so much junk that people would buy on their own, and as consumer researchers wrote more and more books and assumed greater influence in the American economy, it became necessary to develop newer products to be sold here, as well as foreign countries. Our concern for the environment did not exist in the 1940s, '50s, and '60s, and so we thought that it was perfectly alright to destroy rivers, mountain ranges, forests, and the American savannah, all in the name of jobs and stimulating the economy.

However, by the 1970s, we began to see serious problems with the notion of pumping vile, deadly pollutants into the air we breathe, the water we drink, and the soils we farm. With the advent of mass lawsuits in the late 1970s and '80s (asbestos for example, and the anti-tobacco litigation), as well as a growing awareness of the importance of environmental protection, American businesses started shifting their manufacturing to offshore facilities in Asia and Latin America. There, the environmental hazards were less visible (at least, to Americans), and this strategy was successful for a while, but with catastrophes such as the deadly, mass poisoning at a Union Carbide pesticide plant in Bhopal, India in December 1984, and many others, before and after, it became clear to environmentally-sensitive people that conventional manufacturing practices, where dollars came before people's safety, were just part of the game.

As a result, there has been a growing recognition in the United States that our usual way of doing business is no longer acceptable.

---

[79] **Vance Packard,** *The Hidden Persuaders* (Pocket Books, 1957)

Many factories have had to relocate outside of the country, or have shut down altogether, costing many jobs here in the States.

So, we're supposedly protecting the environment, but what can be done to create jobs to replace those lost in traditional industries?

Infrastructure

This is the game-changer.

Instead of creating low-value (but high-cost) goodies and gadgets (hear that, Microsoft, Apple and Google?), perhaps we ought to seriously begin converting our economy in two respects: repairing and innovating in infrastructure, and converting from a hydrocarbon-based to a renewable-energy economy. Why are these such important areas?

There are several reasons why infrastructure and energy-conversion are so vitally needed.

First, from an economic point of view, there are tremendous costs associated with deficient infrastructure. Deteriorating roads, dangerous bridges, electrical and gas systems that don't function at full capacity all the time, or which use too many polluting resources, dams and reservoirs past their useful lives, inadequate or nonexistent internet connections, towns and cities with poor design, traffic congestion, all these things cost the country many billions of dollars in lost productivity.

Second, from the perspective of "pride of place," it's difficult to become excited about driving to and from work at five to seven miles per hour on roads pitted with potholes, cracks, and/or simply too much traffic. It's even more challenging to look forward to driving over bridges which may collapse or experience other problems any day.

Third, and most importantly, the environmental impact of deteriorated infrastructure cannot be overstated. The huge amount of airborne pollution (smog) generated by cars needlessly idling in stalled traffic, from the east coast to the west, and the overall environmental degradation from too many vehicles being built and driven, are major factors in creating an economy with many far-reaching geopolitical landmines.

Add to the economic, environmental and psychological burdens of lousy infrastructure the fact that it adds to health problems from too much smog; adding to global climate change; devastating many parts of the world to get oil, thus alienating people in foreign countries, and it becomes clear that we need to "clean up our act."

Putting people to work in infrastructure repair and innovation is not a quick-fix. This is a public works program that could potentially last for 30 – 50 years, possibly more, and would improve the psychology of communities, states, hell, entire *regions*. Imagine: going to work every day, knowing that you're actually helping to restore America's backbone and muscles, and making improvements in how we live. That gives people a sense of pride and fulfillment, far more than making a web page or soliciting leads for a time-share company or driving Über. Wives could be proud of their husbands, and vice versa, for doing purposeful, constructive work that gives hope to future generations and keeps money in our pockets instead of wasting it on enrichening the "fat cats," such as the Koch brothers, Sheldon Adelson, and their ilk.

Energy Conversion

The demand for oil has created many alliances (and pseudo-alliances) between America and oil-producing countries which has led to wars, terrorism, and the other negative aspects of American foreign policy.

Likewise, we have expanded domestic and Canadian production, using new technologies such as "fracking," to obtain oil and natural gas from fields in Texas, New Yok, Pennsylvania, and in Alberta, Saskatchewan, and Manitoba. We search for coal, tar-sands, and other hydrocarbons to power our cars, trucks, trains and planes; to fuel our power plants; and to make the plastics that destroy our environment and create a plastic "blob" the size of Texas, floating in the Pacific Ocean. The hydrocarbon-based energy economy is simply no longer sustainable if we are to preserve most life on Earth.

Many scientists and engineers have looked into the merits of renewable energy--wind, solar, geothermal, hydroelectric, wave-power, among others--and have concluded that there is much promise from these sources. Obviously, they need to be improved in their efficiency, and there are a number of issues that need to be addressed (storage of electricity, for example), but significant advances have already been made and there are many more to come.

Part of energy conversion requires that we avoid carbon-footprints in obtaining deployable energy, and a related environmental concern is in removing carbon dioxide from the atmosphere and reducing carbon dioxide-based acidification in the oceans, which has been killing coral reefs around the world. This process, called "carbon sequestration," is vitally important because carbon dioxide production from man-made activities is a major reason for the global climate change afflicting our world.

In and of itself, the carbon sequestration industry could create many thousands of jobs in the various sectors in which it would work, e.g., afforestation/reforestation; agricultural practices; oceanic "farming"; biochar; biomass; direct air-removal; and, perhaps most promising of all, the recent development of a process of creating magnesite in the lab, a mineral which naturally absorbs carbon dioxide.[80]

We need a concerted, world-wide effort for the sequestration process to be a complete success, but it must first start in the United States because our per-capita generation of carbon dioxide is much higher than anywhere else.[81]

Of even greater (but less-discussed) significance is the greenhouse gas *methane*. It produces about 20 times more heating influence than carbon dioxide. The problem is that there are huge quantities of methane trapped in the permafrost in Alaska and Siberia. As we suffer from heating due to global climate change, vast amounts of permafrost-locked methane will be released into the atmosphere and dramatically escalate the heating of the earth. It is the carbon dioxide-

---

[80] https://www.sciencealert.com/scientists-make-natural-mineral-magnesite-to-scrub-carbon-dioxide-co2

[81] https://www.ecowatch.com/carbon-sequestration-2461971411.html

based heating which is the catalyst for the release of methane, which is why it's vital that we quickly reduce the amount of carbon dioxide released into the atmosphere, and sequester at least 40-50 million tonnes of it every year for the next 75 – 100 years.

When infrastructure improvements and energy conversion are joint forces, our economy and our environment will both dramatically improve. The two should have a synergetic effect.

The blending of Infrastructure and Energy Conversion would necessarily require an increase in the budgetary allotments for research and development. As pointed out in Chapter 16, the Japanese, South Korean and Chinese governments allocated substantial budgets for R&D. Not surprisingly, these countries now are among the strongest in the world, with dramatic economic growth and improved environments. Not long ago, that was not so, but once basic economic requirements are met, countries can concentrate on more elevated concerns, such as a clean and green environment.

In today's superficially booming economy, it might seem counterintuitive to say that we have a huge unemployment problem, but we do. Notwithstanding the Department of Labor's quarterly statistics, the fact remains that the private sector is not at all invested in improving our infrastructure, and the energy conversion industry desperately needs far more money than venture capitalists are willing to provide, despite its urgent importance. The answer is that the government has to step in and take the lead in infrastructure and energy conversion. It's that simple.

During the Great Depression in the 1930s, President Franklin D. Roosevelt urged Congress to create departments or bureaus that would help with the unemployment crisis, which was averaging 25% (and much more in the industrial cities). Agencies like the Public Works Administration (PWA), the Works Progress Administration (WPA), and the Civilian Conservation Corps (CCC) created jobs and in the process built many structures and landmarks still visible today. Here are a few examples: the Triborough Bridge; Grand Coulee Dam; Hoover Dam; Ft. Peck Dam; La Guardia Airport; the Lincoln Tunnel; the Overseas Highway (linking Miami to Key West); and many others.

"The sheer number of accomplishments is staggering. CCC projects included 3,470 fire towers erected, 97,000 miles of roads built, 3 billion trees planted, 711 state parks created and over 3 million men employed. The PWA funded the construction of over 34,000 projects, including airports, dams, schools and hospitals. The WPA is credited with having constructed 651,087 miles of roadways, repaired 125,110 public buildings and constructed 853 landing fields. From 1933 and the birth of the New Deal to 1939, unemployment dropped from approximately 15 million to 9 million and most of those workers were employed by New Deal programs."[82]

Not only did these folks do important work, but in so doing they regained a sense of purpose and of hope, and renewed their willingness to fight on in the face of tough challenges.

Naturally, people would ask "Who's going to pay for all this work? Isn't the government essentially going to be paying people to work?"

Yes, it will.

The government will advance the monies necessary to complete the initial (and probably the intermediary) R&D financing until such times as promising technologies and industrial conversions are robust enough for commercial deployment. With proper education, financial incentives, and social media encouragement, it may be possible to take the disadvantaged youth of all stripes and persuasions into programs that will bring them up to speed and show them the excitement and joy of doing something meaningful for themselves, their families, their communities, and for the world. Wouldn't that be a powerful legacy?

We can do it, but it requires political will and the ability to articulate a grand vision for the future, where we are not held hostage to Facebook, Instagram, and the myriad other meaningless distractions that keep us from being focused on what is important.

It will take a commitment to a color-blind society, where everyone is given a chance to have a meaningful life and to carry their weight.

---

[82] Bill Holland, *The Great Depression Top Five Public Works Projects of the New Deal* (<u>Owlcation</u>, February 24, 2017)

With the crises facing our society, our world, and our survival as a species, as Bill Clinton used to say: "We don't have anyone to spare."

PART IV
AMERICAN CULTURE, AND OUR PLACE IN THE WORLD

CHAPTER 23
PART OF THE GLOBAL COMMUNITY

We must return America to being a robust, dues-paying member of the Global Community. Yes, we need to exert leadership, but through examples, not merely bold talk. The U.N. and multiple parts thereof; our Peace Corps program; many programs that supported health and human services activities around the world; and funding for (and participation in) global culture activities, would all reestablish the respect once universally held for us throughout the world.

Due to dramatic improvements in international communication, members of Third World or Developing societies are no longer the "frightened little brown people" who were cowed into submission by the "big, brave, white men with guns." National and regional pride play an increasingly-important role in international relations, and we Americans would do well to respect that factor and give it its due.

This may sound like a side-note, but it's not.

I have been puzzled by the incongruity of conservatives (mostly Republicans) supporting Donald Trump and his manifest love of Russia. Conservatives were bitterly anti-communist, and anti-Russian, for the last 70-plus years, so why have they jumped onto the pro-Russian bandwagon over the last three years or so?

I believe it stems from one word: *racism.*

White people in the United States, especially the Southern states, are increasingly worried about our country's changing demographics. Statistics show that America is becoming a "darker" country, with colored people/people of color assuming a greater percentage of the population. By the year 2045, white people will be an absolute minority.

As human beings, we operate on the basis of the "triune brain," discussed at the beginning of this book. Our "reptilian brain" functions have certain profound, unconscious impulses that cause us to have certain attitudes. As people, we:

- Like those who look like us and fear those who don't
- Want to belong to common groups of like-minded people
- Avoid those groups who are different from us
- Develop "reasons" for hating/feeling antagonistic towards those who are different
- Have a zero-sum feeling about others, i.e., gains for others are losses for us.

The history of America, up until the 1960s through the 1980s, has essentially been that of an enclave, where the dominant power has been that of the white male. Once the civil rights movement gained momentum, with television and movies showing more and more non-white actors, there began to be a fear, inchoate at first, that the white people of America were under attack; that they were losing their positions of power and privilege; and that as the country became darker, white people would lose out on the control they had enjoyed for hundreds of years.

American conservatives were particularly worried about this demographic shift, and right-wing talk-show hosts on radio and TV trumped up the worries about demographic losses with dog-whistle, "coded" talk.

Somehow, on an intuitive basis, Donald Trump knew how to appeal to these people and when he started cozening up to Vladimir Putin many in his base liked what they saw. The Russians are a white, European people (according to the video shots played on Fox News), and the fact that Trump liked the Russian leader reassured them that maybe, just maybe, there was an ally that would prevent the overthrowing of white people in America.

In short, the racism seen in Trump supporters (and political conservatives, in general) is based on fear of the loss of a sense of privilege to be white, entitled to power, and having an identity as a people.

Trump's unbelievably-outrageous behavior is overlooked among his supporters because he knows how to appeal to them. His messages, coded for racist sensitivities, harken to an earlier and seemingly more secure day, when America was "a white man's Heaven," where non-whites "knew their place," when they weren't "uppity," and when there weren't challenges to the *status quo*. Blacks, browns, yellows, and reds were second-class citizens, and had to suffer in silence from the oppressive behavior of the White Man. They were generally not allowed to voice their frustration with a system which idealized Freedom and Liberty for All, but practiced *apartheid* in reality.

Our world is racially and ethnically diverse. Of the seven point six billion people on Earth, only one-sixth (1,266,666,667) is white, and the other five-sixths (6,333,333,333) are non-white (Asian, African, Hispanic).

The demographic trends since the end of World War II reveal multiple cultures in the Third World/Developing Countries throwing off the yoke of the "White Man's Burden," i.e., imperialism. Thus, colonies in Africa, Asia, and Latin America have said "We choose freedom," and they have gotten rid of their European (mostly British) and American masters.

In addition to the geopolitical changes, there have been many economic and cultural changes. Many of them derived from the post-War schism between the Soviet Union and America. In order to foster support for their side of the conflict, the Americans engaged in many programs designed to foster economic and cultural development: the Peace Corps, U.S.A.I.D., and many "soft-loan" programs (essentially, grants) to foreign countries in Asia and Africa (including the Middle East). Beyond economic assistance, the U.S. encouraged the development of music, art, theater, and other forms of cultural expression. The combination of monetary and artistic support created a substantial legacy of good-will towards the United States.

Naturally, the Soviets did the same thing to counter American influence. Thus, there was a period of about 40 years (late '40s through the late '80s) where former colonies received attention from rival suitors, and they could play hard to get so as to garner additional support.

By the time of the demise of the Soviet Union, the military industrial complex in America had completely dominated our foreign affairs outlook, and expenditures for non-military foreign aid virtually vanished.

Additionally, in our political spheres, since the time of Ronald Reagan we had George H.W. Bush, George W. Bush, then Donald Trump running the country. Courtesy of the economic disasters resulting from the terms of both Presidents Bush, Bill Clinton and Barack Obama were largely consumed with putting out economic fires on the domestic front.

At least under President Obama there was a brief resurgence of hope that America was no longer the racist, imperialistic power it once was. However, not much money was made available to Obama for non-military use overseas due to Republican Congressional intransigence. Nonetheless, Obama was able to get the United States to join in the International Climate Accord in Paris in December 2015, perhaps the biggest accomplishment of his two terms as President.

The tone of the Trump Presidency has been unambiguous: whatever progressive legislation there was (or Executive Orders signed by Obama) had to be undone, the sooner the better. The key ingredients to American foreign policy under Trump are a return to the imaginary world of unadulterated American hegemony over the rest of the world and a view that America is the greatest country ever.

It goes without saying that such a path is completely unavailing to us. Due to American ignorance (willful or otherwise), we are locked in a false perspective that believes the rest of the world is in a dependency relationship with us, and hangs on to every word we utter. What our present political leadership does not hear is the laughing at the ridiculous position into which we have put ourselves.

We have a narcissist-in-chief who knows nothing about science, technology, engineering, or math; who is ignorant of geography; and lacks any understanding of or appreciation for any cultures, histories, or values different than those he thinks are "American." For Trump, a prototypically-insecure schoolyard bully, "might makes right," and he thinks that America is unique in its ability to project domineering force around the planet. He is willfully ignorant of the military power in the hands of Russia and China, and thinks that our having 11 supercarriers and eight assault carriers that are bigger than the aircraft carriers of virtually any other navy is tantamount to being able to dominate any other military in the world.

Throwing out his chest in his usual buffoonish way, Trump has ignored the dramatic threat increase from the Chinese navy; has alienated four allies we need in the Western Pacific (Australia; the Philippines; South Korea; and Japan); has cozied up to Chinese President-for-Life Xi; and has entered into dangerous waters by starting a trade war with China that can only ramp up hostilities between the two countries.

Trump makes matters worse by failing to understand the mentality of the Russians. They have a 1,000-year history and they have a bone-deep love of "Mother Russia." Russians will die, every last man, woman and child, to defend their homes. Russians can be a very warm and hospitable people---but do not make the mistake of attacking them.

The Russians have been pursuing a STEM-centric education model for many years, and their children are <u>smart and well-educated</u>. Elementary school kids there often are far smarter than college graduates here in the U.S. Isn't that a shame?

Because of the poor quality of our news, Americans have no idea of the dramatic improvements made in all sectors of the Russian military over the last 18 years since Vladimir Putin first took office. He inherited a country on the brink of collapse and has transformed the economy; the educational system; the R&D facilities; and the military into world-class competitors, not just of the U.S. but with other countries as well.

The U.S. Congress has instituted a program of imposing economic and other sanctions on Russia. Congress has thought that in so doing it would punish Putin and his regime. Again, American ignorance would be laughable if it didn't have such serious consequences. U.S. commentators have spoken about how the sanctions will hurt the Russians, but they fail to understand that the Russians and the Europeans are being brought closer together as a result. The sanctions imposed on Russia actually forced it to become more self-reliant in terms of producing foodstuffs and consumer goods, as well as to increase trade with Europeans. The real effect is that the U.S. has wound up hurting itself by alienating its European allies and damaging its own export markets.

It is to be hoped that the American electorate will increasingly understand how we need to change our ways of dealing with other nations, and other cultures. If the electorate does, we should see a dramatic shift in American foreign policy and practices that will:

- Dramatically increase economic support for challenged countries
- Focus on radical environmental transformation, and with technology-sharing agreements
- Result in major improvements in our immigration laws and policies, and
- Increase support for various cultural exchange, medical benefits, and democracy-producing programs

As we help to make this a better world and create conditions where people *want* to stay where they were born and raised, we can generate a great deal of good-will all over the planet. No longer will they think we are simply a nation of greedy imperialists trying to steal their national patrimonies.

When we do these things, people around the world will see that finally, *finally*, America has awakened to its responsibilities as a global leader, and is practicing, at last, what it has been preaching for so long.

One final part of America's legacy is its adventures into space. We need to **return to space**---and **not** through the insane proposal of the creation of a "Space Force," which would militarize space and lead to a complete waste of our resources. The Air Force is already meeting our defense requirements and a Space Force, as a sixth military branch, would be a duplication of the resources already devoted to the Air Force. It would also violate the 1967 Outer Space Treaty.

Many good things came out of our involvement in space. New technologies; new learning/ educational techniques; new ways of thinking; the Internet; personal computers; and a spirit of international cooperation all arose from our space program. Returning to the cooperation mode instead of adverse competition would do wonders for our planet, for cross-fertilization based on different perspectives would help us to achieve our goals and meet common needs for the sake of mankind, rather than providing a gigantic ego-boost for us.

In short, it's time for us to grow up and do some positive things as a contributing member of the global community.

CHAPTER 24
ART, CULTURE, AND STANDARDS

The Arts

Many people call for us to restore funding for the arts. What good does it do a people to have material abundance if it has no soul? Arts provide that soul. It is imperative that we reinstate, richly, music, theaters, sculpting, painting and other forms of personal expression in the schools. Give kids healthy ways to express themselves and learn vital social skills.

We have seen a huge increase in *graffiti* over the years. In many instances, this explosion in defacing public or private property reflects emotional/psychological disturbance on the part of the *graffitists*. Many of them are angry about whatever traumas they have been through---being homeless, unloved, the product of a broken home, what-have-you---and they have to vent. We need programs that will catch the so-called "artists" and get them the help they need. The billions of dollars of damage they cause every year could be dramatically reduced by appropriate remediation programs.

Giving kids constructive ways of expressing themselves can accomplish many wonderful things. Imagine teaching them to channel their negativity into positive action. Imagine showing them how to turn negative energy into something that will help others and give meaning to their lives. I think that many times, the *graffitists* lack the ability to use words to express their feelings, so they strike out in the only way they know how. The problem is that there's a cost associated with this inarticulate venting, so they have to learn how to talk and think with words to express themselves.

Music is vitally important. It teaches social skills. It imparts the values that the group goal is more important than the ego-gratification of the sole performer. It instills the notion that people function better by cooperating than by competing, and more benefits arise from cooperation than competition.

Culture

Culture is not merely the collective body of tastes in the arts, but is also the reflection of manners generally accepted as the identity of a group of people, how they go about living their lives, raising their families, and the goals to which they aspire as a society.

From World War II up to about 1970, we had a culture in this county that was much more homogenous than it has been over the last nearly 50 years, or was for about 300 years before the Second World War. This "cultural diversity" stemmed from several factors.

As analyzed in Chapter 13, historian David Hackett Fischer traced the origins of four distinct waves of English immigrants to this country, each with its own unique characteristics. Fischer described their story and cultures as "the origins and stability of a social system which for three centuries has remained stubbornly democratic in its politics, capitalist in its economy, libertarian in its laws and individualist in its society and pluralistic in its culture."

These distinct cultural groups gave rise to the divisions persisting in American white society today: the New Englanders/Yankees (Puritans) coming from East Anglia; the Cavaliers and indentured servants went to Virginia (and their gentry created the Southern states' plantation culture); the Quakers went to the Midatlantic and the Midwest; and the Irish-Scottish and borderlands people (near the border with Scotland) who went to the West and to the South, and whose ranching and agriculture traditions overlapped.

These folks stubbornly held on to their family and clan traditions literally from the mid-1600s to about 1945. Only in the crucible of World War II was there a significant coalescence into an "American" identity, when unity was absolutely necessary if American military personnel were to have a chance against their enemies. This cultural overlap lasted up until the late 1960s, but things changed during the 1960s, and disrupted and eventually destroyed our homogeneity.

We know that the 1960s was a time of massive social transformation. The anti-war, Civil Rights, and Women's Rights movements were huge factors, forcing people outside of those groups to look at their calls for being treated with dignity and respect, legal equality, and with a place at society's table. The hippies' life-styles and some of the radical political groups, along with religious groups, espoused "do your own thing" philosophies. Many authors and "self-help" gurus crawled out of the woodwork and started entire self-help industries, which continue to this day. The net result was a society in which the libertarian philosophy of "do your own thing" was restored to the height of personal ethics for many people.

Demographics in particular have shifted from 1970 to the present. Blacks and Asians have not increased their percentage of our country's population by any appreciable degree, but the Latinos have definitely assumed a major increase in population, and with them added to the black and Asian populations, they will be a minority majority by 2045, according to the U.S. Dept. of the Census.

Standards

Regardless of ethnicity or race, I believe it is vitally important for Americans to forge an identity as one people, with a focus on doing the *right* thing rather than "do your own thing." This involves a commitment to political democracy; economic justice; and a strong belief in supporting the Bill of Rights.

None of this has anything to do with race, ethnicity, gender, or country of origin. But these are matters that need to be taught in homes from early childhood so that they become engrained in people as soon as possible and so that we can once again learn what it's like to be "Americans" without the hyphenated prefix in front of that word.

Tattoos, Piercings, Strange Haircuts

Many kids think that tattoos, piercings, unusual haircuts and hair-dying are good ways to distinguish themselves and "make a mark." Many teenagers are trying to separate themselves from their parents and think that a tattoo (or group of tattoos) will help accomplish that. They often don't think about possible health risks; how they will think about the tattoo in five, 10, 30 years; and the very real danger of employers stereotyping them for having tattoos.

Parents need to start the conversation with their kids early—maybe around eight, nine or 10—about making themselves "stand out" by developing their own identity. How do they do that? Not by what they look like, but by their actions, their choices, the decisions they make. Those are the lasting reflections of who they are—and they don't have the negative consequences of having to get rid of a tattoo or piercing that they may later regret having gotten.

The Addictive Cellphone

Another problem area is in the addictive use of cellphones. In so many parts of society—walking down the street, being in a restaurant, waiting in line, we are so alone, so *isolated*, by the very device that is supposed to connect us with other people. Again, parents need to get kids focused on conversation, face to face, and interacting with one another in person.

Respect for Authority

Among the most important cultural traits we need to reinstate is internalized, active respect for authority. This means parents *have* to learn how to be parents. Don't let your kids call you by your first name. There has to be a hierarchy within the family, the first social unit the child with which the child interacts. Society is made up of people; people are primates; and we have millions of years of primate evolution which made us live in hierarchies in order to survive. We cannot just blithely ignore that reality.

Much of today's anti-authoritarianism comes from two sources from the 1960s, and one source from today.

During the 1960s, the Civil Rights movement and the Anti-War movement both caused people to seriously challenge the authoritarian *diktats* of older, white Establishment males, who tried to enforce Jim Crow-era racist laws and traditions, on the one hand, and the orders to fight in the Vietnam War, on the other. Progressives felt that it was time for a change in social *morés* and laws as to race and that we needed to get out of a war that was causing such cleavage in American society. The numbers of young people who died in Vietnam came to over 58,000 but the damage to our respect for authority has lasted to this day and has impacted a huge part of our culture.

Stemming from the anti-anti-war crowd (mostly Appalachians and their descendants in the country-western sphere of society), which had a long history of distrust of authority and government, there has been a current (i.e., within the last 25 years) orientation to chest-beating "do your own thing" from the right wing. This attitude has filtered down to kids over the last generation or so, and it is this spirit which has triggered a whole new appearance of "scene kids," those with a panoply of tattoos, piercings, and weird hair colors, along with an amalgam of "emo" and Gothic attire.

They send a message of emotionally-damaged young people with serious self-image problems.

You might say, "But what about the hippies with their weird hairstyles and bell-bottoms?" I would say that those things can be changed, and there was no permanent alteration to one's appearance or personality. With tattoos, piercings, and earlobe plugs, however, these changes are permanent and appear to reflect patterns of self-loathing.

When I was in high school, one of my favorite teachers taught AP History. He was a repository of wise sayings. One of his best was:

"Everyone is free to swing his fist, but the freedom to do that ends precisely at the point where my nose begins."

If I don't like something I read or hear on the radio or TV, I can read something else, or switch (or turn off) the channel. In today's society, however, youngsters have not been taught that there are social consequences to their behaviors, so in public I am forced to look at people with freak-show physical appearances (tattoos, piercings, bizarre hair colorings) and/or hear their bump-a-thump-a "boom-box" music coming out of cars and/or boom-boxes on the sidewalks or the subway or areas of the mall where I might want to shop.

This is not the case of an elderly "geezer" yelling out: "Hey! You kids! Get off my lawn!!"

This is the case of millions of people being forced to watch and/or hear degenerate images and/or music when we don't choose to see and/or hear it on our own. In short, why should I be forced to watch people with disgusting appearances, who lack the social respect to restrain themselves in public?

You might argue and say: "Well, this is just part of the ongoing 'culture war' that's afflicted our society for many years. Get over it." I, in turn, would say: "Who gives these people the moral right to force me, and countless others, to watch the parade of 'uglies' and be compelled to listen to so-called 'music' that I don't like? Why am I, and countless others, required to be their audience?"

The real problem is the lack of standards, where people are taught that what they say and do have social consequences and that they need to subordinate their own self-absorbed impulses to the greater good, so that people feel that they are members of and belong to their society.

The need for standards is clear. If we do not have an identity to which we can claim allegiance, to a group to which we belong and which wants us, then there will be a sense of dissociation, of loneliness, of isolation, and, ultimately, of despair. Is that the legacy we want for ourselves or to leave our children? I don't think so.

Conversely, we must also understand that the individual's rights and talents must also be respected and enhanced. But, in Aristotle's quote at the beginning of this book, "…Society is something that precedes the individual. Anyone who either cannot lead the common life or is so self-sufficient as not to need to and therefore does not partake of society, is either a beast or a god."

EPILOGUE

THE MAIN GOAL OF THIS BOOK is to provide specific guidelines to help people improve where and how we live. This is not at all about creating arguments between "the Left" and "the Right," or this group or that group. It's about learning how to live together and volunteer together to strengthen our weaknesses, to make us a better people.

As social animals, we need societies in order to survive. Sadly, American Baby Boomers have been brainwashed into adopting an individualized *ethos*. The result is that the *anomie*, or lack of moral standards, of social control and regulation, has created a Balkanized society where we pursue our own, or our communities', agendas rather than focusing on common goals.

We have looked at history because in order to know where we are going we first have to understand whence we came. As financial planners are required to say, "past performance does not guarantee future results," but among those of us who study human behavior we can safely predict that people "go with what they know." Unfortunately, what most of us know is the old "reptilian brain" way of dealing with the world. We need to get away from that pattern if we are to survive as a species.

Our history as a people is relatively short. We had four distinct English cultures which provided a basis for our early, pre-Revolutionary country. Additionally, we had Germans, French, and Spanish, as well as other countries' immigrants coming here in the 1700s and 1800s. The Italians, the Chinese, the Irish, the Japanese, the Polish, the Scandinavians, and the Russians added to our voluntary immigration pool. The kidnapped, enslaved blacks from various parts of Africa were not exactly enrollees in a Club Med tour, but they played a huge part, nonetheless, in creating the American culture.

Prior to the identity politics of the 1960s and '70s, we had people who were identified by the names of the countries from which they came: Germans; Poles; French; Italians; Irish; and the like. They made great efforts to assimilate, to learn the language, to adopt to our style of dress and all the social *morés* that make a culture. For them, America was a "melting pot."

After the time of identity politics, we adopted hyphenated names: African-Americans; Cuban-Americans; Chinese-Americans; and the like. Now, many of the people whose first language was Spanish do not bother learning English, or adopting to our *morés*. This creates a real problem because the people who were here before the Spanish-speaking arrivals think they should learn English and "act American."

This can be a real problem due to the Sapir-Whorf Hypothesis, which posits two fundamental principles, namely:

Speakers of different languages:
- Perceive the world differently
- Have different cognitive systems

Accordingly, the mental universe of an English speaker is different from that of a native Mandarin (or Spanish, or Russian, or German, etc.) speaker because they use different languages, with different structures, vocabularies, forms, and grammars.

If we do not mandate that people learn to speak and write (and eventually *think*) in English, then we will have further difficulties in understanding one another. Without understanding, it will be impossible for us to unite as a people, and without unity, will we be able to fulfill the mandate of America?

In closing, this returns us to the central question of this book: what can we do to improve our world?

There is "Plenty" for us to do to make life better. Let's get started!

Appendix
Resources

The following lists the names and websites of many charitable, non-profit organizations, organized by category. With a little research using duckduckgo.com, you can add to this list, based on your own interests.

Advocacy Groups for Human Rights and Civil Liberties
These charities help people fight for their rights, either through legal advocacy or by providing education, awareness, and funding for human rights initiatives.

- American Civil Liberties Union

- American Jewish World Service

- Americans United

- Americorps

- Amnesty International

- Anti-Defamation League

- Association on American Indian Affairs

- https://www.bnaibrith.org/

- Children's Defense Fund

- Coalition to Stop Gun Violence

- The Carter Center

- Center for Constitutional Rights

- Committee for Missing Children

- Doctors of the World

- Human Rights Watch

- NAACP

- The Center for Victims of Torture

- Committee to Protect Journalists

- Center for Community Change

- Experience Corps

- Indivisible

Animal Rights

Animal rights organizations seek to protect animals and their habitats through advocacy, as well as, action-based and educational initiatives.

- African Wildlife Foundation

- American Humane Association

- American Association for the Prevention of Cruelty to Animals (ASPCA)

- Animal Legal Defense Fund

- Animal Welfare Institute

- Best Friends Animal Society

- Born Free USA

- Defenders of Wildlife

- Doris Day Animal League

- D.E.L.T.A. Rescue

- Dian Fossey Gorilla Fund International

- The Elephant Sanctuary in Tennessee

- Farm Sanctuary

- Friends of Animals

- Humane Farming Association

- Humane Society of the United States

- Marine Mammal Center

- National Audubon Society

- Performing Animal Welfare Society (P.A.W.S.)

- Pet Partners

- RedRover

- Wildlife Conservation Society

- https://www.worldwildlife.org/

Land Conservation and the Environment

These charities seek to protect the environment through education and conservation initiatives. Charities in these categories may focus on research, direct action, or political and legal advocacy.

- https://350.org/

- American Farmland Trust

- American Forests

- American Rivers

- Appalachian Trail Conservancy

- Beyond Pesticides

- California Environmental Justice Alliance

- Carbon Fund

- Center for Biological Diversity

- Chesapeake Bay Foundation

- Coral Reef Alliance

- Cousteau Society

- <u>Earth Island Institute</u>

- <u>Earthjustice</u>

- <u>Environmental Defense Fund</u>

- <u>Farm Aid</u>

- <u>Greenpeace</u>

- <u>Keep America Beautiful</u>

- <u>National Park Foundation</u>

- <u>Ocean Conservancy</u>

- <u>Safina Center</u>

- <u>Sierra Club</u>

- <u>https://www.sunrisemovement.org/</u>

General Emergency Relief

These organizations step in and provide relief during difficult times such as natural disaster and war.

- <u>American Red Cross</u>

- <u>Children's Disaster Services</u>

- <u>Emergency Nutrition Network</u>

- <u>Firefighters' Charitable Foundation</u>

Refugees

These organizations provide support for people forced to flee their homeland due to war, famine, political unrest, disease, and natural disaster.

- <u>American Near East Refugee Aid</u>

- <u>American Refugee Committee</u>

- <u>International Rescue Committee</u>

Medical Assistance

These programs provide medical relief and assistance to people who may not otherwise have access to affordable care for financial, social, or geographical reasons. These organizations may also provide emergency medical relief.

- AmeriCares

- Catholic Medical Missions Board

- CURE International

- Direct Relief International

- Doctors Without Borders

- International Medical Corps

- Medical Teams International

- Operation Smile

- Samaritan's Purse

- World Medical Relief

Education, Research and Cultural Preservation Groups

These groups have specific missions geared towards improving education, providing more educational opportunities, promoting cultural awareness, or preserving the culture of specific populations.

- ACCESS College Foundation

- Africa-America Institute

- AFS USA

- American Enterprise Institute

- American Indian College Fund

- Asia Society

- https://www.attendanceworks.org/

- Building Educated Leaders for Life (BELL)

- Hispanic Scholarship Fund

- Scholarship America

Health: Research, and Education
These health foundations focus on research about specific illnesses.
Many also have an educational component to enlighten people about
prevention and management strategies.

- amfAR

- Alliance for Aging Research

- American Heart Association

- American Stroke Association

- Arthritis Research Institute of America

- Avon Foundation

- Breast Cancer Research Foundation

- City of Hope/Beckman Research Institute

- Epilepsy Foundation

- ALS Association

- American Diabetes Association

- Autism Speaks

- Hearing Health Foundation

- Juvenile Diabetes Research Foundation

- Lupus Research Institute

- Brain and Behavior Research Foundation

- First Candle

- March of Dimes

Support for Chronic Illnesses and Diseases
These organizations provide financial, emotional, or medical support for people with chronic illnesses and their loved ones.
- Alzheimer's Association

- American Kidney Fund

- American Leprosy Missions

- American Liver Foundation

- American Lung Association

- American Parkinson Disease Association

- Arthritis Foundation

- Bailey House

- CaringBridge

- Cystic Fibrosis Foundation

- Easter Seals

- Huntington's Disease Society of America

- Project Sunshine

- The Sunshine Kids

Cancer Support and Research
These cancer charities provide research and support for people with cancer and their loved ones. Support may include education and emotional support.
- American Brain Tumor Association

- American Cancer Society

- BreastCancer.org

- Cancer and Careers

- CancerCare

- Cancer Recovery Foundation

- Cancer Research Institute

- St Jude's Children's Research Hospital

- Children's Cancer and Blood Foundation

- National Children's Cancer Society

- Children's Cancer Research Fund

- Jimmy Fund (Dana-Farber Cancer Institute)

- Livestrong

Support for Physical and Cognitive Disabilities
These charities provide financial support, education, and research for people with physical and mental disabilities, as well as their families.

- Achilles International

- American Action Fund for Blind Children and Adults

- American Association of the Deaf-Blind

- Christopher and Dana Reeve Foundation

- Heritage for the Blind

- The ARC

- United Spinal Association

Poverty
These organizations help the economically disadvantaged around the world with an array of programs such as education, advocacy, health care, housing, and anti-hunger programs.

- Catholic Charities USA

  http://www.catholiccharitiesusa.org

- Catholic Relief Services
  http://crs.org

- Christian Appalachian Project
  http://www.christianapp.org

- Christian Relief Services
  http://www.christianrelief.org

- Coalition for the Homeless
  http://www.coalitionforthehomeless.org

- Lutheran World Relief
  http://www.lwr.org

- Modest Needs
  https://www.modestneeds.org

- Oxfam
  https://www.oxfamamerica.org

Feeding the Hungry

These charities fight hunger around the world by providing food, clean water, and funding.

- Action Against Hunger

- Africare

- Bread for the World

- Care

- City Harvest

- Farmers and Hunters Feeding the Hungry

- Feeding America

- Feed My People

- [Food Bank for New York City](#)

- [Society of St. Andrew](#)

Promoting Self Sufficiency

These charities help people help themselves through education, micro loans, and similar initiatives.

- [Accion International](#)

- [Agros International](#)

- [National Relief Charities](#)

- [Bowery Residents' Committee](#)

- [Brother's Brother Foundation](#)

- [Center for Community Change](#)

- [Dress for Success](#)

- [FINCA International](#)

- [Food for the Hungry](#)

- [Habitat for Humanity](#)

- [Heifer International](#)

- [Wings of Hope](#)

Impoverished Children

These charities help children around the world who live in poverty by providing food, medicine, and education.

- [All God's Children](#)

- [Cambodian Children's Fund](#)

- [Children's Hunger Fund](#)

- [World Villages for Children](#)

- [Children International](#)

- ChildFund International

- Compassion International

- Covenant House

Senior Citizens

These charities provide advocacy, education, and research for senior citizens.

- AARP Foundation

- Bright Focus Foundation

- National Council on Aging

- OASIS Institute

- Seniors Coalition

Supporting Military and Veterans

These charities provide support services for those who serve our country, as well as their families. Services may include financial assistance, mental health care, and veterans services.

- Adopt a Platoon

- Air Force Aid Society

- AMVETS National Service Foundation

- Armed Services YMCA

- Army Emergency Relief

- Blinded Veterans Association

- Canine Companions for Independence

- Disabled American Veterans Charitable Service Trust

- Paralyzed Veterans of America

Supporting Fire Fighters and Police
These organizations provide advocacy and support for the civil servants who keep us safe.

- American Association of State Troopers
- American Federation of Police and Concerned Citizens
- Law Enforcement Legal Defense Fund
- National Fallen Firefighters Foundation
- National Law Enforcement Officers Memorial Fund

Watchdog Groups
These organizations make sure public organizations like the government and the media are operating appropriately and with honesty and integrity.

- Accuracy in Media
- Center for Responsive Politics
- Citizens Against Government Waste
- Citizens for Responsibility and Ethics in Washington
- Common Cause
- Government Accountability Project
- Judicial Watch
- Media Research Center

Children and Youth
These charities support youth in a variety of ways, from providing constructive youth activities to advocating for children's rights.

- Big Brothers Big Sisters of America
- Boy Scouts of America
- Boys and Girls Clubs of America
- Camp Fire

- Cedars Homes for Children

- Child Find of America

- Child Welfare League of America

- Girl Scouts

- Junior Achievement

- KaBoom!

- National 4-H Council

- National Center for Missing and Exploited Children

- SADD

Women

Women around the world face unique issues such as discrimination, domestic violence, and human trafficking. These charities support various women's initiatives.

- Catalyst

- Equality Now

- Family Care International

- Global Fund for Women

- International Planned Parenthood Federation

- League of Women Voters

- National Organization for Women

- National Network to End Domestic Violence

- Women Employed

www.ingramcontent.com/pod-product-compliance
Lightning Source LLC
Chambersburg PA
CBHW071602030726
47593CB00001BA/280